CH

My Chosen Trails

D1457634

DISCARD
MAY 2003

WESTMINSTER PUBLIC LIBRARY
3705 W. 112th AVE.
WESTMINSTER, CO 80031

MY CHOSEN TRAILS

A Wyoming Woman's Recollections
through the
Twentieth Century

Verna Burger Davis

Deep Creek Press
Golden, Colorado

MY CHOSEN TRAILS

Copyright © 1998 by Verna Davis
All rights reserved, including the right of reproduction
in whole or in part in any form.

Library of Congress Catalog Number: 98-96028

ISBN 0-9663347-0-1

Printed in the United States of America

DEEP CREEK PRESS
25608 Sunrise Lane
Golden, Colorado 80401
Ph.303-526-7220
Ph/Fax 303-234-1391

Book design by Amy Martin and James Davis
Cover design by James Davis

FORWARD

"With a light heart and great expectations," wrote this incredible lady as, in her '90s, she began another new adventure--the writing of this book. That phrase expresses her attitude throughout a lifetime of adventure that progressed from a simple pioneer beginning through three generations to a modern life as she experiences it today.

Music was a wonderful thread that bound together most facets of her life. Love and admiration, respect and genuine affection for her abundant and diverse family and friends, and especially for the children she taught through many years, were the other binding forces that helped make her life both fascinating and complete.

The reader expects, at the beginning, to plod through a myriad of day-to-day details, but suddenly and unexpectedly, a unique word, phrase, or sentence expressing a fresh idea leaps forth from the page. These surprises may be hilariously funny, or introspective, or philosophical, but they lead the startled reader to muse: "I wish I had thought of saying it that way."

The theme throughout the book gradually and eloquently leads up to the last few paragraphs that culminate in the poignant question posed by the author, now nearly 96 years old: "How about a return to the 'Age of Reason' for the 21st century?"

J.D. Love
March 7, 1998

ACKNOWLEDGEMENTS

I wish to express my deepest appreciation and thanks to my son, Jim Davis, and my granddaughter Amy Davis Martin for helping make this book possible. They spent countless hours at their word processors and on the phone conferring with me as they proof-read, edited, selected and placed pictures and otherwise got the manuscript ready for the printer.

My three children, Jim, Dorothy, Allison and their families never wavered in their constant encouragement that spurred me on to complete the manuscript.

Thanks also to Dr. J. D. Love, a Wyoming pioneer in his own right, who kindly took time from his active life to review the manuscript and write the Forward. Margaret Wilde Meyer carefully edited the copy to provide another level of proofing.

Jim designed the cover and map and conducted negotiations for the final product.

Verna Davis, March 1998

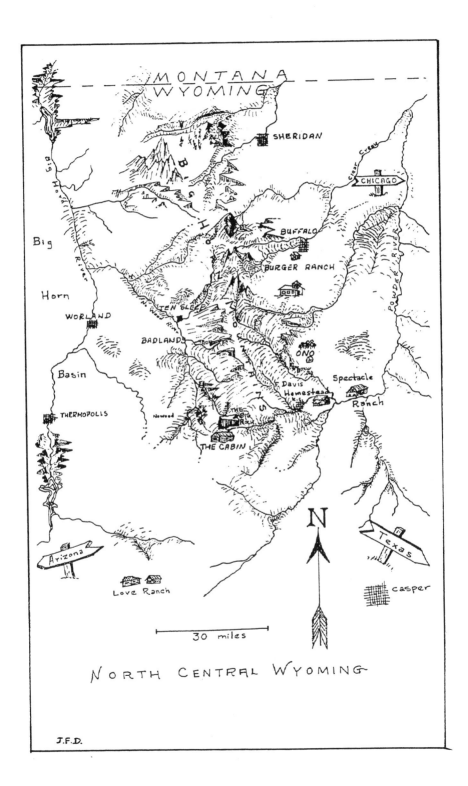

MONTANA

WYOMING

SHERIDAN

CHICAGO

Clear Creek

Big Horn River

BIG HORN

Big

Horn

BUFFALO

BURGER RANCH

Basin

WORLAND

TEN SLEEP

No Wood River

BADLANDS

ONO

POWDER RIVER

THERMOPOLIS

Nowood

Davis
Homestead

Spectacle
Ranch

THE CABIN

Arizona

Texas

N

Love Ranch

casper

30 miles

NORTH CENTRAL WYOMING

J.F.D.

To Jim, Dorothy and Allison

In Memory of
Frank Davis

"The dreams of childhood...its airy fables, its graceful, beautiful, humane, impossible adornments of the world beyond; so good to be believed in once, so good to be remembered when outgrown"
                                                                    --Charles Dickens

Chapter 1

My Early Years

One July day in 1902, my father hitched up his team to a light wagon and, when other preparations were completed, took off for Buffalo, Wyoming. He, my mother and their young son Lawrence were coming from their ranch on the Powder River below Kaycee.

After a strenuous two day journey, they arrived at their destination at the Stockman's Hotel where mother was to await the arrival of their second child. She didn't have to wait long, as I was born a month early - not surprising considering that 60 mile trek over dirt roads in a wagon whose only shock absorbers were the springs under the wagon seat.

My father, Leonard Ulrich Burger, was born in Oregon, Missouri to Ulrich and Christina Kaltenbach Burger. Ulrich Burger was born near Berne, Switzerland and Christina was born in Bonn, Germany. My mother was Nellie Winingar Burger, daughter of John W. Winingar, born in Virginia, and Martha "Mattie" Cowman Winingar, a native of Iowa.

When I was about four years old and a third child, Melvin, had arrived, my parents decided to dispose of the ranch and move into Buffalo where Dad had purchased a

home. It was more than just a physical move for my
father, as it also meant a change in occupations. He gave
up sheep ranching and went into masonry. It was quite a
change, although he had had some experience in building
before coming to Wyoming.

I am sure it wasn't hard for my mother to adapt to
the new lifestyle. She loved people. We had a close
neighbor who she enjoyed visiting, and her brother Fred
and his family also lived on the same block. Our house
was comfortable and not too far from school.

Mother had her fourth child, Marland, before I
started school. Lawrence and I started school the same
year. I suppose this was in order to keep each other
company going to and from school that first year.

Burger family - Leonard & Nellie with (l. - r.)
Verna, Lawrence and Melvin, 1904

It is hard to distinguish between what we actually
remember of our childhood and what we have heard

others discuss, but some things do stick in my mind. In the first grade we sat in small chairs around a table. I can remember an embarrassing moment when my little chair tipped over and I tumbled to the floor exposing my home-made flour sack bloomers! One of the boys laughed. That little incident didn't change my attitude toward school though.

I loved my teachers - Miss Hunt, who gave us a sense of security and comfort the minute she walked into the room, and Miss Ellis, the music teacher. Today we would call her a shot in the arm. She would come bouncing in with a bright smile on her face and in no time would have us all belting out "Good Morning to You" at the top of our lungs - and meaning it!

Buffalo was a very stable town. The citizens were people who had businesses which the town's future depended on. The cattlemen were the biggest contributors to the early economy; their investments were such that they were bound to stay a number of years in order to make their businesses pay. Buffalo still has many descendants of those early pioneers who had started businesses in the beginning.

The very nature of the early day businesses in this part of the country created many problems. The big cattlemen, with their unbounded free range, had things their way for some time. Then came the first thorns in the cattlemen's side - the homesteader and the sheepman. They mixed with the ranchers like oil and water.

The invention of barbed wire, the Homestead Act, the cattle rustlers, and the constriction of the free range all contributed to troubles between the different factions, making for a most colorful and dramatic regional history, from the Johnson County War to the Ten Sleep Raid. These and related events seemed to create a unique atmosphere in and around Buffalo. Even today just mentioning the Johnson County War still stirs up interest in many circles.

We children were so fortunate to grow up in an environment of national peace and more or less serenity. I do not recall any worrisome national problems being discussed at home. That is, not until 1914 and World War I. The theme, as I look back, seems to have been *PROGRESS*! Not in making money, especially, but progress in the comforts of living. My dad made the first concrete sidewalk in town, just one item in the beginning of providing a more comfortable life for the Westerners who had roughed it for so long.

Our entertainment was simple and self-made. Montgomery Ward was a great boon at Christmas time, and at the beginning of the school year when our wardrobes were replenished, at least to a small degree.

In the spring, the Fields Garden catalog soon became well worn as we pored over the mouthwatering illustrations. In fact all catalogs were popular items; we fought over who was going to look at them first. Not that we were going to buy anything, but the illustrations were marvelous to our eyes. Not having many magazines nor any television or movies, the magnificent array in the mailorder catalogs of everything from booties to buggies, and corsets to cookstoves sent us off to never-never land.

At Christmas time we were allowed to make messes all over the house by stringing popcorn and cranberries and making paper chains with colored paper and flour paste, all of which would adorn the Christmas tree, along with a dozen or so candles that were lit under the strictest supervision of our parents. On Christmas morning we all piled out of our beds at the earliest possible hour. I might add we were deterred somewhat by the cold house, but it warmed up quickly after Dad was ready to do his part and make a fire in the big stove in the sitting room (today we would call this the family room). There wasn't a stack of packages under our tree - everything was in plain sight or hanging on the tree. What we saw was what we got! I think I was grown before I saw Christmas wrapping paper.

Battery operated toys were unknown; the only mechanical toys I remember were little tin animals or clowns that would shuffle along on wheels after being wound up with a key like a clock key. One year I received a little cast iron cookstove complete with grate, reservoir to keep water hot, and a stove pipe. It was about ten inches long. We thought it a rare treat when my girlfriend Margaret and I were allowed to make a real fire in it, outdoors of course. That stove now sits on my bookcase, and in recent years my granddaughters were allowed the same privilege with that little stove when they visited me.

Dad had constructed a large building in the back of our lot. It contained a drying area where he seasoned his cement blocks. Above that was an attic plenty high to stand up in and which was well floored. In one end of that room Margaret and I had our play house. Mother showed us how to make doll furniture cut from cardboard and folded. Last year's catalogs supplied curtains, pictures, and anything else our imagination would allow. We spent hours up there in the summer when it surely must have been sweltering, but we could care less. At least my brothers didn't bother us there.

Verna & Margaret, 1916

Our first car was a brand new Model T Ford, complete with side curtains and shiny brass headlights lit with acetylene gas which had to be ignited with a match. As time went by we graduated to a new Studebaker which sported two little jump seats that pulled out from the front seats and faced the back. We made many journeys which would be considered just short jaunts these days, but we felt like we were on quite a tour at the time.

Our favorite trip was out to Grandmother and Grandfather Winingar's Red Cliff Ranch, a wondrous place of imagined mystery forests, family warmth, and treasured things - but more about that later.

Music lessons were an important part of my growing up, and I shall be eternally grateful to my parents for the sacrifices I'm sure they made to enable me to take music lessons for so many years from Mrs. Kennedy. She was an attractive gray-haired lady who, I heard much later, had a rather colorful past in the history of Buffalo. Sometime in her life she also had received excellent musical training, for she taught me techniques that stood me in good stead when I studied at music schools in Chicago.

We didn't have much excitement in our little village, but one spring we had a terrific flood. Debris piled up against the Main Street bridge, causing water to flood up as far as Gatchell's Drug Store. What a heyday all the kids had when they were allowed to go downtown and paw through the mud covered merchandise at the New York Store, then the local department store!

I remember the stiff but handsome purses we girls proudly carried around while we were playing house. Our mothers took advantage of the sales following the flood and bought yards of material which were subsequently, in my case, converted into one of the nicest wardrobes I ever had.

A new and higher bridge was built across Clear Creek by my dad, as well as an extensive retaining wall along the creek next to the Occidental Hotel, which prevented a reoccurrence of such a disaster. The cobblestone wall is still there, bordering the normally crystal-clear creek.

One of my father's bigger contracts was to build a power house and dam five or six miles west of Buffalo. H.P. Rothwell had the franchise for furnishing electricity for the town, and this was to be his source of power.

As far as I know, when Dad got ready to build it he just took his crew up there, dammed up the creek, and started construction. No waiting around for EPA or DEQ approvals. Mr. Rothwell did the feasibility study and was also his own engineer. It was a beautiful area at the site of the dam and the power house, a stately structure which still stands by the side of Clear Creek; it is a mute reminder of the ingenuity of the town's early citizens.

Powerhouse Dam on Clear Creek

Occasionally mother would pack a lunch for some of us kids and we were allowed to spend the day with Dad in the canyon. What a treat that was! We could run free all day without Mother continually cautioning us to "Stay off those big rocks, you might fall off!" or, "Stay away from the creek, you might fall in!" Dad thought we were old enough to take care of ourselves. Of course we had to prove him right so we could go again.

Mother never learned to drive a car, however she was a very good horsewoman. We had acquired a horse named Duke along with a one-seated buggy, and this conveyance provided transportation for some of our most exciting excursions. A lunch was prepared and we would literally pile into the buggy and off we would go. Our destination was usually up Clear Creek near the mouth of the canyon. The boys would probably fasten a string to a willow pole and fish a little. Mother would wander around collecting wild plants and flowers. I preferred a more sedentary pastime, and usually selected a shady spot and read.

Children of today are considered quite privileged with their televisions, sophisticated transportation, computers, and a chance to take part in organized games from the time they are very young. Well, maybe! When we were kids the youngsters in the neighborhood would bring over their picture postcards and watch them being projected big as life onto a screen by means of our Magic Lantern which Dad brought home one day.

In school we had exciting competitions in math when the winner was the one who worked his brain the fastest - without the benefit of a calculator or computer. The nearest thing we had to organized games was when children from all over the neighborhood would gather under the street light and play "Run Sheep Run," "Kick the Can," or "Hide and Seek."

Those of us who lived in the first half of the 20th century were to see mechanical, scientific and economic developments that have essentially changed our lifestyles and philosophies. We saw the first automobiles, the first plane to fly over town, the first crystal radios, the first television, the first computers and, in fact, improved methods of doing everything.

When we were growing up everyone was encouraged to raise more, make more, to dig, drill, chop, mine, and produce all we could in as short a time as possible. The modern generation is a different story, as they are obliged to follow more restrictive laws for environmental protection, speed limits, harmful substance control, and sharing of natural resources. We now have to control production in order to protect our natural resources.

One could say our philosophy has almost reversed itself as far as production, if not consumption, are concerned. The next 100 years will be interesting.

Chapter 2

At Grandma's Place

It was a warm day in early summer. My three brothers, Melvin, Lawrence and Marland, and I were moping around trying to think of something to do. "What a great day to go to Grandma's!" No question about it, we all agreed on that. If only we could persuade our dad to drive us there. It was 30 miles of unimproved roads and our conveyance was a Model T Ford with side curtains that kept out only a small part of the dust. "You ask him!" we all said at once, but after a few moments of discussion it seemed the logical thing for me to do it, as I was the only girl.

I found our father in his favorite summer place, relaxing in the chair swing on the front porch enjoying a much deserved rest after a week of heaving heavy loads of cement and gravel in his work as a concrete contractor. I didn't think of that, however, when I suggested that it would be so nice to take a trip out to see Grandma and Grandpa. After expressing what I think is assumed reluctance (he adored his wife's parents, as they did him), he finally said, "Well, go ask your mother if she wants to go."

"Oh, my goodness. I have so much to do." was her reply, but by that time all four of us were clamoring for her to hang up her apron and take the day off. Soon we were told to wash our faces and put on clean clothes, which we did in record time, and were out in the car waiting impatiently for her to tidy up the house a bit and get a few necessities for an overnight stay, as it was too long a trip to make for one day.

At last, after filling the car with 15¢ gas, we were on our way. Our top speed was 30 mph, but we had to slow down for every turn in the road in case another car might be coming from the other direction - there was mostly one set of well-traveled ruts. The rough roads kept us from getting up much speed to climb the hills, and by the time we reached the top the Model T would be chugging and whining in low-gear at a walking pace.

Then, six or seven miles from the ranch we had to open gates - there must have been at least five. That, together with our impatience to get there, made that last stretch seem interminable. Finally we were through the last gate and we kids were all literally hanging out of the car windows trying to be the first one to spot the white gable of Grandma's house as we chugged over the top of the last hill.

As long as the Winingars lived on that ranch they never had a phone, so they didn't know when company was coming. I suppose they were always hoping that we would show up, but were nonetheless happily surprised when we did. When we drove up to the yard gate here came our beloved Grandma, wiping her hands on her apron and at the same time dabbing at her eyes. Right behind her were Uncle Jesse and Uncle Harry beaming their surprise and welcome as well. Grandpa, being a little more laid back, got up from his easy chair in time to meet us at the door.

John & Mattie Winingar, 1927

Father and Mother seemed to be much more compatible in the presence of our grandparents and uncles than they were at home, where even at a young age I sensed a feeling of disapproval between them. Not particularly of each other's actions, but in retrospect I believe it was somewhat a censure of each other's judgment, which became more evident when some of my brothers developed some rather worrisome habits.

Grandma's house was a veritable wonderland to us. We marveled at everything and immediately made a quick excursion through the house to see if all the treasures were still there. They were. There was the little hand painted dish that sat on the piano, the marvelous paper weight with the pretty scene inside that became a snowstorm when turned upside down. There were the awe-inspiring pictures in the photograph album with the brass clasp that lay on the center table. I looked again and again at those likenesses of our ancestors, I admired the beautiful clothes they wore - all the tucks, lace, gathers, insertions, and the myriad of buttons. I learned later that every stitch was done by hand. No wonder women were house bound in those earlier days. The hairdos were no less elaborate. All the waves and curls had been accomplished with the aid of the old fashioned curling iron which was stuck down into a lamp chimney over the flame until it was hot enough to sizzle. I don't recall seeing any teeth in the entire album! No smiles - I guess that generation had a horror of being considered frivolous, thus the stern expressions.

Another object of our interest and fought over use of was the platform rocker, a burdensome, unattractive chair that sat on a platform with rollers that allowed the chair to move back and forth, requiring some effort on the part of the occupant.

A major attraction was the Edison phonograph, a square wooden console about the size of a word-processor. On top was a spool which revolved when the machine was wound up with a crank on the side of the box. A cylinder-shaped record was slid onto the revolving spool, the needle placed on the record, and then we thrilled to Sousa's band blaring out in all its glory. On one of the march records the music faded in at the beginning and faded out at the end. In our mind's eye we could see those horn players in their uniforms coming into sight then watch as they went out of sight down the long street. Another record I remember was "The Preacher and the Bear," a dialogue done by some comedian which sent us into spasms of laughter every time we heard it.

The ranch house at Red Cliff had three bedrooms, plus a fold-out couch in the dining room. We youngsters slept on the floor in the dining room. I remember going with Grandma to a corner cupboard in her bedroom where she had stacks of quilts which she had pieced together out of old clothes, filled with wool or cotton bats and tied with yarn. One or two of those under us and one over us made a most comfortable bed. The nights were chilly as the altitude was probably near 6000 feet; by early morning the house was cold and it felt good to have the quilts pulled up over our heads.

No one had to drag us out of bed the next morning as we were all up early and eager to get out and do some exploring. The smell of coffee and fresh baked biscuits whetted our appetites as we all gathered around the table. Grandma gave me my first ever cup of coffee, answering my mother's look of disapproval by saying, "Law, one cup of that won't hurt her. I watered it down." However I must say I never pursued the habit after we got home. I really think it was not that Mother thought the drink itself was harmful to my health, but that she thought giving children something that gave adults so much enjoyment bordered on the immoral!

We all enjoyed breakfast. There were always little episodes and special things that made each meal memorable. I recall a silver teaspoon beautifully engraved with a life-size strawberry on the handle. Grandpa told us that it had been a bonus with his last can of tobacco. To preserve the peace we had to reluctantly agree to take turns using it.

We need to go back a few years to find out what it was that drew the Winingar family to this, or at least what was then, rather remote area of Wyoming. The family had come from Nebraska to Cheyenne where

Grandpa did carpenter work. The family also had a connection there - John Phillips was in the area raising horses and selling them to the government. The Winingars called him "Uncle Johnny," although I don't know whether he was actually a relative. Uncle Johnny had a contract to deliver horses to Fort McKinney, an Army cavalry post near Buffalo. The primitive road at that time was no more than a wagon trail that followed close to the mountains from Mayoworth to Buffalo.

Grandpa Winingar hired on to help with the horse drive. Grandpa later wrote a beautiful letter to a niece in Indiana describing the beauty of the area where they had stopped for a night. He said in his letter, "As I view this beautiful and peaceful valley from my vantage point here on the side of the mountain, I vow I shall come back here and build a home." And that he did, taking up a homestead on the remote foothills of the Big Horn Mountains.

Red Cliff Ranch, 1926

They chose to build the ranch buildings in a lovely little valley through which runs a small, tree-bordered stream. The creek rises clear and cold at the base of the steep mountains immediately to the west, and flows through the sedate setting of my grandparent's homestead. To the north a thick grove of quaking aspen trees was my childhood enchanted forest - a mysterious or even dangerous woods where one might encounter a wolf! To the east a fair-sized hill crowned by a long, bright red sandstone bluff gave the ranch its name. There was adventure and beauty in every direction

While my brothers and I were tearing around from one attraction to another that morning, our folks were active in the culinary department. A couple of chickens were beheaded, dressed and cut up ready to fry. A cake in the oven was nearly ready by the time we young ones had returned from our excursions.

One of the men dug out a couple of chunks of ice from the insulating sawdust in the ice house, put it in a gunny sack, and pounded it with the flat of an ax until it was in small enough pieces to pack into the outside part of the ice cream freezer. Salt was mixed with the ice to make the process colder. By the time we responded to the dinner call, the cranking of the freezer was well under way. It was a great privilege to turn the crank until it became too hard for us to manipulate. It was then turned over to the uncles.

Our job then was to take turns standing on the freezer to keep it from wobbling as the mixture of cream, sugar, eggs and vanilla became more frozen. We would hang onto someone's shoulder for dear life during this climactic operation. Then came the really fun part. The dasher was slowly removed from the ice cream container and placed in a large bowl. With spoons we rapidly cleaned off the ice cream still clinging to the paddle blades. The bites were small, but Oh! were they good. The container of ice cream was packed in ice and salt to await the finish of the dinner.

Climaxed with cake and ice cream, the dinner was finally over and sadly it was soon time to start the long trip back to Buffalo. We were all exhausted on the trip back, but came alive when someone shouted, "There's McBride Hill!" Our faithful little Ford put-putted up that last incline and over the top. We were on the downhill stretch to home, still full of dinner and a fairy tale book full of memories.

During subsequent visits I made to Red Cliff Ranch, I observed many other oddities that I am sure could be found at other ranches, but at the time I thought were peculiar to only Grandma's house.

With the help of the boys, Grandma made an annual ritual of whitewashing the entire interior of the house. Whitewash was made by mixing lime and water. In its liquid state it is rather caustic, so it must have given my grandmother, who was a model of sanitary housekeeping, a feeling of assurance that no critters were left alive after the periodical treatment.

Another illustration of her immaculate housekeeping was the way she did her laundry. The water source was the very cold stream that tumbled out of the mountain and had been diverted towards the house through a wooden flume which terminated in a miniature waterfall. A bucket set under that would quickly fill up with the most delicious water that we thought ever came out of a spring.

The water was very hard though, and on wash days a copper boiler tub was filled and put on the stove to heat. Pure lye was added to soften the water, the scum that formed on top was skimmed off, and the wash water was ready. After scrubbing everything on the washboard, the laundry was rinsed in clear water and bluing was added to give the clothes a whiter look.

In addition to all this, the dish towels were put back into the lye water, left in the boiler, and actually boiled with an occasional stirring with a broomstick, until every vestige of stain had disappeared. They were then hung out on the clothesline for the sun to finish the bleaching. Even the most brilliant colors had a much softer shade after this treatment!

This same stream that furnished household water ran through an opening in the spring house, a room built on the north side of the kitchen containing a concrete basin constructed to hold four or five inches of water before spilling out the east end and back into an irrigation ditch. In this cool room Grandma kept her milk, cream, cottage cheese (of which she was a master), meat and leftovers. Her buttermilk was out of this world, so said lovers of the brew. As for me I never learned to like it.

One of Grandfather's favorite evening snacks was clabbered milk to which he added nutmeg and sugar and ate with a spoon. Speaking of Grandpa, another of his little habits I always watched with delight was the way he would light his pipe by sticking a twig from the wood box into the fire in the cookstove, getting a miniature flame going at the end of the stick, and lighting his pipe with it.

One time when I was spending a few days at my favorite place, I decided to venture into my mysterious woods by myself. I hadn't gone far when I spied a lovely bunch of purple violets growing by a damp log. I scurried from here to there looking for more. Before I knew it I had reached the far edge of the grove of trees and was out in the bright sunlight. I couldn't believe it; I had been so busy searching for flowers that I had not been afraid, but now I came face to face with the realization that I must go all the way back through that dark and forbidding forest all by myself to get home! I kept my eyes straight ahead as I hurried back in a more direct route than I had come. In no time at all I was on the other side with Grandma's house right there. My mysterious forest had suddenly shrunk from that treasured vision in my mind, and one of my childhood illusions was shattered.

Horse Creek Canyon near Red Cliff Ranch

I had always wanted to go up the hill east of the house and be able to actually touch the Red Cliff, so one day when my friend Margaret and I were spending a week at the ranch we felt adventuresome enough to attempt the trek up the hill. Uncle Harry gave us each a nail so we could carve our names in the soft sandstone of the bluff. The last 20 feet to the base of the cliff was quite steep, but we were determined to make it. We carved our initials near the many others on the rock wall. Many of them were in such fancy script that we weren't too proud of our crude attempts, but we were recorded for posterity anyway.

In the 1880's when the Winingars first settled on their homestead next to the mountains, the main road between the upper Powder River and Buffalo more or less followed the base of the Big Horn Mountains. The Ono Post Office was established at the Red Cliff Ranch along with a wayside stop, with Grandma as the postmistress and proprietress of the way station. Grandma - Martha was her name - was popular with young and old alike, and everyone knew her as "Aunt Matt."

Several years later, when the road was moved further east, the post office and way-station were closed, but the Winingar house didn't close its hospitable doors. I know of at least four young men who, unable to find work, ended up at Red Cliff Ranch where they knew they would be welcome, even though my grandparents were having a difficult time making ends meet. Usually there would be only one boy at the ranch at a time, and he helped feed stock, chop wood, or perhaps hunt game to restock the larder. A couple of these free boarders told me much later that those months at the Winingar ranch were among their happiest memories.

Uncle Jesse joined the Marines in World War I. He was in a training camp in Pennsylvania when the war ended. He lost no time in getting back to Buffalo and making his appearance at the home of his sister, my mother. He was so handsome in his Marine uniform that we all stood and gawked at him. We must have seemed quite countrified to him since he had just traveled all over the civilized eastern United States. However suave he might have wanted to appear, he could not hide his eagerness to get back out to his old stomping grounds at Red Cliff.

My dad told him to wait until Saturday and we would take him out. Now that trip was easier promised than accomplished. For some reason my father rented a team and buggy from the livery stable to make the trip. Perhaps our car at the time was not deemed capable of making the long trip. Of course we all had to go along - Dad, Mother, Jesse, four half-grown kids and a baby. I remember that it was a cold November day; we were all bundled up with warm rocks at our feet.

When we stopped at the first gate at Willow Glen, not far out of town, Jesse got out to open the gate. The wind took his Marine cap off and sent it bounding across the prairie faster than you ever rolled a hoop! It took some effort by my dad and Jesse to catch it. We could hear them laughing their heads off as they approached the rear of the buggy.

This gaiety continued all the way to the next gate. Here they both got out to open the gate, and spent a few extra moments at the rear of the buggy to "check the wheels." When they resumed their seats, they had even more hilarious dialogue. This condition intensified with every gate, and by the time we were through the last one Dad and Uncle Jesse were convulsed with mirth. We kids had never seen either of them so funny, and were laughing as hard as them. Mother knew what was going on even if we didn't, and the harder we laughed the more grim her expression became. By the time we arrived at the ranch she was hardly speaking to anyone. Of course the mirth was helped by the contents of a flask supplied by Jesse, and I later thought that Mother should have been more tolerant of Jesse's celebration. After all, he had come through the war with no more serious calamity than falling in love with a city girl from Pennsylvania!

Sometime in the twenties two of my brothers, Marland and Melvin, were successful in building a crystal radio receiver that would pick up a station from Chicago. I was away from home at the time, but had a report later from Arliss Hoover, a distant cousin who was spending the year at Red Cliff. She wrote that as she and the Winingars sat around a fire one cool fall evening, they heard a car coming. A visitor at that time of the day was unheard of, and it was with more than a little apprehension that they waited for the arrival of the unknown travelers. It was with great relief when the two grandsons walked in with that crystal radio. They set it up and got only a little faint scratchy music, but enough to keep at it. Grandma and Arliss went to bed but the others stayed with it well past midnight.

The next morning was spent talking over the wonders of the age as they leisurely drank their coffee. In retrospect I have concluded the priorities at that wonderful place of my grandparents were what made it so appealing. Pleasure came before duties! On this particular morning the cattle were waiting patiently by the fence for their hay and cubes that didn't arrive until well into the afternoon.

That seemed to be indicative of my grandparent's philosophy - they just wanted everyone around them to be happy. In short, they weren't very good business people, and the cattle and land business was becoming more competitive. Grandmother was the driving force, but didn't have much to do with the business end. The inevitable borrowing, some bad judgment in buying some eastern cows, and the depression resulted in insolvency and the ranch going into receivership in the 1930's. I doubt if Grandmother really knew the state of affairs out there before she died at the ranch in 1934. Grandfather had passed away several years prior to that.

The boys, Jesse and Harry, gradually drifted away to other jobs, and the place passed on to other owners. It is presently owned by someone who bought it for a hunting lodge. I have not visited there for over 60 years, but the memories of those of us who spent time there in those wonderful years are priceless. Though they lost the ranch, the legacy our grandparents left to heirs and friends is worth more than an empire of land.

Chapter 3

Transitions

In 1917 a group of teenagers, all agog with excitement, trooped up the hill to enroll as freshmen in Johnson County High School. During the next four years we would learn something about independence, initiative, competition and self-discipline, as well as some general academic knowledge that would take us somewhat beyond the boundaries of the three R's.

There is not much similarity between the high school of today, with its well-equipped art and music departments, highly organized sports, and high-tech laboratories with computers, and the simple curricula of the early part of the century.

Instead of athletic sports that required teams, we concentrated on physical training. Our equipment consisted of Indian clubs, wands, hurdles, and parallel bars and rings. We performed some rather intricate exercises with those sawed-off broomsticks called wands under the direction of the English teacher. Running and jumping required no equipment, so we did a lot of that.

Evenings after school some of the boys could be found down at the baseball park (now Prosinski Park) practicing football under the tutelage of the volunteer coach who owned a clothing store downtown. I don't remember that we ever had anything but interclass games. The uniforms, I must say, were not very uniform, as most of them were concocted at home using lots of cotton stuffing.

My brother Marland played football and became so well known for the way he charged his opponents that he earned the nickname Bear, which he went by for the rest of his life. One day after he had graduated he was watching some high school boys practice, and when the coach wasn't happy with their lack of aggression he told Bear to "Get out there and show 'em how to tackle!" Bear charged through a tackle and broke through the board fence that surrounded the playing field. After high school he played football for the University of Wyoming for a couple of years.

The girls in their voluminous black bloomers could be seen at the same time in the gym playing basketball (girl's rules), which was much more restricted than the game today. There was no music program, but Jim Gatchell, a local druggist who played the violin, organized a little orchestra in which I played the piano. I loved those after-school sessions, although, as far as I know, the public was never made aware of our talents. There were no school buses. Practically everyone who lived in town walked. Many country kids who didn't drive boarded in town during the week.

No hot lunch was served at school. We either took a sandwich in a paper bag or ran home to eat. Our family lived on the corner of Lott and DeSmet, east of the present hospital. We thought nothing of hurrying home to that welcome bowl of homemade potato soup or whatever Mother had waiting for us. There was a narrow swinging bridge across Clear Creek, just west of where the Burritt Street bridge is now. There were few buildings between the creek and our house, allowing for a fairly straight path across vacant lots to reach our destination.

Burger residence, Lott and DeSmet

During our freshman year Charles Wilkerson and I were elected to the newly formed Student Council. We felt pretty important when the superintendent stuck his head into the large assembly hall, which served as a study hall for the entire student body, and said, "Verna Burger and Charles Wilkerson, report for Student Body meeting." I must say though, that we stood slightly in awe of the more sophisticated upper classmen, and I am sure it was well into the year before we were brave enough to stand up and make a modest proposal.

Most of us have had teachers who stand out in our memories. Miss Edna Gherken, a serious but excellent science teacher, was one of mine. She impressed upon us that scientific statements should be considered as theories and not final conclusions until proof was irrefutable. She taught us that science is a never ending field of experiments with great possibilities for discoveries for the open-minded student. At that time some texts referred to the atom as being the smallest particle of matter. Miss Gherken countered that theory by suggesting to us that the atom could be split into smaller components, thereby releasing tremendous amounts of energy.

Another of our memorable teachers was Mrs. Mary Holmes Watt, a beautiful lady who introduced us to classical literature, a new experience to most of us then. Today's children are introduced to the works of famous American and English authors at an early age through many mediums, but sometimes miss the experience of reading the actual texts. Be that as it may, Miss Holmes taught us to appreciate the power of words.

Miss Mildred Eschrich attempted to guide us through the intricacies of hand sewing. Sewing machines came later, but our class, Homemaking, used the needle and thread, and were taught the running stitch, the blind stitch, and if we wanted to be fancy, the cat stitch. Along with these simple lessons, Mildred impressed upon us the importance of neatness in sewing, accuracy in cooking, and did her best to break us of our haphazard habits in those fields. We were taught the importance of thoroughness and the satisfaction of completing a project. The school kitchens were equipped more elaborately than those in most of the students' homes.

Then there was Mae Norval, one of those rare persons who made the inadequate feel adequate, the slower-than-normal kids feel smart, and the unattractive feel beautiful. Thus, everyone had a feeling of confidence instilled in them. Through her example, we all learned a great sense of values.

Verna in 1917 Studebaker

During our four years in high school, we were reminded in several ways of the importance of planning for the future. For most of us, graduation meant the last of free education, and of our carefree life at home. If we were going on to school, that meant we would need money, which meant getting a job. Girls were much more limited in their choice of employment in those days than they are today. Boys could work as janitors, paper boys, farm help and other manual labor.

The top priority of jobs for girls was teaching. We heard of several openings in rural schools. Six weeks of summer school at the University in Laramie would provide us with a one year certificate, and it looked like a great opportunity to get that needed money to go on to college. Consequently, the summer of 1921 found several of us taking off on our first independent adventure, to the University of Wyoming.

Getting there was no small feat as practically no one had cars, or at least one that would make that rigorous trip of 300 miles. We rode the train, nicknamed Duffy's Bluff, from Buffalo to Clearmont, some thirty miles to the east towards Gillette, then changed trains and on to Hastings, Nebraska, changed again then back into Wyoming and on to Laramie. If you look at a map you will understand why it took more than a day to make the trip that today takes five hours by car!

We were met at the Laramie train station and transported along with our baggage to the campus. There began another first, dormitory living. We had experienced slumber parties which lasted for one night, but to live with one girl, and put up with each other's housekeeping for six weeks? We managed fine, with no disagreements that I can recall. Learning to cope with new situations away from home was part of our education.

In high school we had to get used to a different room for each subject. Now we found it a bit confusing to have a different *building* for each subject. During the summer we took concentrated (a semester squeezed into six weeks) courses: psychology, methods, as well as reviews in primary subjects, all of which would hopefully give us an idea of how to conduct a classroom.

I had been offered a job as the teacher at the Simmons Ranch School about halfway between the Ramsbottom and Simmons ranches, forty miles south of Buffalo. The two weeks following my return from Laramie were spent preparing for my move to the country. I was always excited when I could look forward to a different experience, a new trail into the future. The coming year was certainly that.

I boarded at the Simmons Ranch, a white, two-story frame house devoid of color inside and out. The rocky, steep slope on which the house was built discouraged any kind of landscaping. The interior of the house had snow-white plaster walls. The plaster was made on the site by burning gypsum, abundant in the area. The burned product, plaster of Paris, made lovely smooth plaster. The floors were bare, white lace panels covered the windows, and the furniture was nondescript. The kitchen too, was sparsely furnished and had no running water or drain.

Simmons Ranch

My room followed the same scheme: white walls, white curtains, white bedspread, white table (no dresser); a few nails driven into the wall near the door provided places to hang my clothes. In spite of this Spartan setting and style of living, I have the most fond memories of this warm and generous family. They treated me as one of the family, so I adapted quite rapidly to the inconveniences which they accepted as commonplace.

My two students were Stella Simmons, a 5th grader, who walked to school with me every day (a two-mile hike across the barren mesa), and Bernice Ramsbottom, who walked almost as far from the north. Our little log schoolhouse was situated at the bottom of a big hill which we had to climb every evening to get home.

The girls were models of decorum, so I had no discipline problems. It might have added a little zest had they been more friendly. They never talked to each other as friends. Both were quite shy, and, I learned later that feelings between the two families were not exactly amicable. I regret that I did not have the experience or training to know what to do with two little girls who were without joy or imagination, and spent their days so seriously on schoolwork. Of course, with such a small student body it was out of the question to consider any festivities for holidays, so those days went by with scant notice.

Simmons Ranch School

It was indeed a red-letter day when Margaret Smith, the County Superintendent, came by to pay her official visit. She brought her sister Mary Langhorst with her. They drove to the Ramsbottom ranch, left their car, and walked on to the school. They brought their lunch and spent the day. Margaret could see that I found it difficult making the day interesting for my students. We had few distractions, so lessons and assignments were finished with time to spare.

Margaret suggested we spend the last period of the day doing art or crafts. I planned a simple sewing project to work on. Stella loved it, but Bernice had a sort of nervous disorder and was unable to hold a needle without her fingers shaking. She had trouble doing any kind of artwork requiring coordination of her fingers. Nowadays, perhaps she would be able to get professional help from educators. She was an apt student as far as subject matter was concerned, as long as it required little writing or pictures to be drawn. I had not seen her for twenty-five or thirty years when she came to see me while I was visiting my mother in Buffalo. Her nervous disorder was no longer evident and she had poise, a stylish appearance, and a positive outlook on life.

One day we had a little visitor who gave all three of us a few delightful moments. A pack rat poked his head up through a knothole in the floor. We remained very quiet to see what he would do. He spied a pencil lying on the floor, picked it up in his mouth, and tried to get back through the knothole, which he soon found to be an impossible feat. Nonetheless we set a coal bucket over the hole that evening to prevent any further excursions and requisitions while we were gone.

We had a humongous pot-bellied heating stove which kept the air warm only in its proximity, so we would drag our desks up as close to the heat as possible.

In the wintertime walking would have been all but impossible had it not been for Stella's brother George, who rode his horse to the school house and back to break the trail through the deep crusted snow. I never quite figured out why they didn't just let Stella and me ride the horse ourselves.

As spring approached, we were rewarded richly on our daily treks with the appearance of the first blades of green grass, mayflowers and little yellow buttercups, along with the first welcome song of the meadowlarks and other birds. A very happy day it was, though, when I packed my trunk and departed the ranch for the summer. It was good to get home and back into circulation with my friends and family. In the fall I moved back to spend my second year of teaching in the same place, with the same people, and with the same circumstances.

The Simmons boys, Clarence, Albert and George, were kept busy with their cattle operation. They also had several pet deer in a high pasture near the house. The deer put on quite a show as they reared and pawed at the fence while George was getting their cow cake (molasses flavored cubes) ready to toss over the fence.

An important component of the Simmons' home was music. Edgar Simmons was an expert fiddler. I believe he knew every quadrille, jig, polka and schottische ever written, and he played them with perfect rhythm. His son George was more of a violinist and leaned more toward the current popular music. He didn't read music, but learned to play by ear by listening to records. He produced a beautiful tone from his instrument, and I loved to accompany him and his dad on the piano. Of course they were in great demand at country dances, the most popular form of local entertainment at that time.

The neighborhood, outside of the family, was perhaps the most important entity during the early part of the century in Wyoming. The families who made up the rural neighborhoods were closely knit and their concerns were for the community rather than national events or big city problems. A major reason for this was that communication and travels did not often go much beyond their immediate realm.

Entertainment was a concerted effort. For a country dance someone provided the place, or a country schoolhouse was used. Someone could always be counted on to furnish the music and everybody brought food. Since those functions took lots of effort, the participants made them worthwhile by planning all night affairs, with a meal served at midnight. The wash boiler would be on the stove, full of water, waiting for someone to toss in the coffee that was tied up in little cotton bags. The floor would be sprinkled with cornmeal to make gliding easier, the fiddler would tune up, the caller would clear his throat, and the festivities were under way.

After being fortified by the midnight feast, the dancers were ready to go until dawn made it light enough to harness up the horses and start for home. A designated driver was not needed, as the horses knew where they were going while the passengers dozed.

While I was at the Simmons' ranch, I partly paid for my board by giving Stella piano lessons. In later years she played the piano for her father and brother all around the Buffalo country.

The following year the Simmons School was closed and the girls were sent to other schools. I accepted a school in the eastern part of the district called the Wright School. After the miles we walked to and from my former school, this was a sinecure as the schoolhouse (a one-room shack) was about fifty feet from the Wright home where I stayed. We also were on the Buffalo to Kaycee highway, so I got to go home more often. Dad was building a bridge over Powder River and he would pick me up when he went home for weekends. He had recently purchased a house on High Street, where we lived for ten years.

At this school I had only one pupil, Russell Wright, for most of the year, so I still didn't have a chance to test my abilities. I let Russell go at his own pace, which was a remarkable one. He was reading third-grade books by the end of his first year.

The Wrights were originally from Ireland and had lived in Chicago prior to coming to Wyoming. Mr. Wright had been a streetcar conductor in the city. Mrs. Wright was purely a city girl. They both had to make terrific adjustments when they moved to the dry farm in Wyoming. Their abode was comfortable, but far from modern. One of their neighbors, Mrs. Pratt, in her neighborly way, taught Mrs. Wright how to cope with the inconveniences and unfamiliar ways of the West.

As many a writer has pointed out, the schoolmarm was the romantic focal point of the community. Young women were always scarce in the early West. I seemed to be no exception and had the honor of entertaining several swains during the school year.

One of them, about ten years my senior, came over one spring evening and asked me to marry him. I felt quite honored to be chosen by someone who had resisted the wiles of others for so long, so I accepted his ring.

It just so happened that this man, Bruce, was working for my father on his bridge job. One weekend at home while we were out in the yard, Dad said to me, "Verna, it would mean ten years more to my life if you'd drop Bruce." Since my dad was not in the habit of giving me advice in regards to my suitors, I figured that he must have a pretty good reason for this comment. Also, my alternative plans came to mind, plans I had dreamed of for so long - going to the Chicago Musical College. Nothing was going to prevent me from doing that, especially since I had saved my money for three years to that end. So I broke the engagement and returned the diamond ring.

Verna on her way to a dance

The ensuing summer was a busy one as I prepared for at least nine months away from home. Plans were made through the Chicago Musical College for my entrance and for boarding facilities, as we didn't know a soul in the city.

Finally the day of departure arrived; I was ready to board that "little train that could," Duffy's Bluff, which would take me on the first leg of a journey of my own big adventure.

Chapter 4

Chicago

It was September of 1923. My 21st birthday was the previous July, but my coming of age status didn't affect me a whole lot. I had pretty much made my own decisions since I had graduated from high school, however my most recent decision was a big one.

My determination to further my musical education had never wavered from the time my piano teacher had set a goal for me when I was quite young. At any rate, here I was with my faithful trunk and extra bags ready to board the little train, which I did after a rather tearful goodbye to my family who were there at the Buffalo depot *en masse* to see me off. I sat looking out the window as the familiar landscape disappeared from view, then I turned my attention to my more immediate surroundings.

Across the aisle from me was the only other woman passenger. She was well-dressed, fortyish and had a professional air about her which aroused my curiosity. Before I had a chance to say anything, she asked where I was going. When I told her, she said Chicago was also her destination.

During our subsequent conversation I learned her name was Ella Desmond. She had been to Buffalo, not to see anybody, but to visit her brother's grave. He had been a druggist in the early days and was engaged to Ethel Hesse, who died at an early age during a typhoid fever epidemic. Desmond had requested that, upon his demise, he be buried beside her. His tombstone may be seen today in the Hesse lot.

Miss Desmond proved to be my mentor and guide all the way to the city. She told me what to expect - enormous crowds; what to look for - Red Caps; and what to do - have my destination address ready, have the Red Cap call a cab, and be on my way. True to her prediction, the minute we got off the train at Union Station she was immediately swallowed up in the crowd, and I was on my own. The Red Cap I chose was extremely helpful, although I am sure after one look at me and my luggage he was not expecting a huge tip. As we were making the transition from the train to the cab, I was getting my first impression of the big city.

Union Station - what an enormous edifice: the beautiful domed ceiling, the unbelievable height of the walls, all in beautiful colors. Even the floor was a work of art. The noise was deafening to my country-trained ears. Noise, I learned, was a big part of Chicago. I had never seen so many people. Back home we would recognize each one as a person, but in Chicago they were just collective masses of people.

I marveled at the ease with which the cab driver manipulated his vehicle through those crowded streets. I craned my neck to see what I could of the city sights as we whizzed by. The only preparation I had of what to expect were black and white prints in the newspapers. I was amazed and awed at the real thing - the unbelievable height of the buildings, the hordes of people, and the constant noise of trolleys and trains. I was thrilled with it all!

After driving on more streets than I'd seen in my lifetime, we drew up in front of a stately red stone building whose steps came right down to the sidewalk. My baggage and I were deposited at the front door, and the cab driver was quickly on his way. Living arrangements for me had been made through the Chicago Musical College, where I would shortly begin my musical education.

I was greeted by the matron of the house whom I liked immediately. She was an attractive motherly sort whom, I am sure, had the ability to size up a new tenant quite accurately. I was shown to my room and told when to come down for dinner. This old Victorian house was one of several built quite closely together along Prairie Avenue. They were former homes of wealthy and prominent businessmen of early Chicago. Most of these buildings now housed businesses.

The *Country Gentleman* was published next door. On the other side lived one of the original dwellers, Mrs. Pullman, widow of the train sleeper inventor, who adamantly refused to move.

Our "Working Girls' Club" was furnished elaborately on the first floor with old fashioned but beautiful furniture, long dark red velvet drapes at the tall, deeply-recessed windows, luxurious flowered rugs, and a graciously appointed dining room where we were served a delicious meal that first evening.

The house mother, or matron, held weekly sessions, usually just before dinner in the rather austere sitting room. This lady was not austere, but was firm and positive as she gave out bits of advice which I suspected were aimed largely towards the "babes in the woods" - like me. That and the close association with the more experienced girls at the club soon had me feeling much more at ease in the city.

The Chicago Musical College was within walking distance of the club on Prairie Avenue. I started out that sunny autumn morning with just a little trepidation as I knew not what to expect.

After taking care of the necessary paperwork at the desk, I was directed to the sixth-floor lounge, a very large room furnished with the most ornate and magnificent carved furniture I had ever seen. All of the furniture was painted gold, and the straight-backed chairs and settee were upholstered in rich, red velvet. None of this presented an invitation to loiter. However, I did sit in one of the chairs just outside the small studio with its closed door, behind which I could hear the candidates trying for various piano instructor scholarships. The more I heard, the less confident I became, as they seemed to rip through arpeggios, chromatic runs and tremendous chords with the greatest of ease.

By the time my name was called, my confidence was at low ebb. Nevertheless, I tried to keep my calm when I finally took those thousand steps (or so it seemed) to that piano bench with those stern eyes watching me all the way. I went through a movement from a Beethoven sonata - quite woodenly, I am sure. I was so intent on playing the right notes that the piece sounded more like a chant than a piece of music. Mr. Gordon Wedertz, the teacher I had chosen, proved to be most compassionate. I was accepted and told to report for my first lesson the following Monday.

By Monday, I had somewhat regained my composure and likely had a more confident air when I walked into Mr. Wedertz's studio which was large enough to accommodate a grand piano and an upright piano. One wall was covered with framed photographs of former students, attesting to his popularity.

I sat down at the piano with a feeling of great excitement and anticipation, but was hardly prepared for my mentor's first statement. "Well, you *are* alive, although your playing really didn't indicate as much."

From then on, I came to realize that music isn't just a series of notes, chords, intervals and measures, but that every piece of music has a message which may be brought out by the performer through touch and expression.

In any case, Mr. Wedertz must have thought I had the ability to improve - I certainly had the room to do so. He offered to give me two lessons a week instead of one. Along with piano, I took harmony - a study of intervals, major, minor, augmented and diminished, and their proper succession. This was taught by a serious spinster-type lady who never once challenged the rules set down by Mr. Marriot, the writer of our text book. I should like to have known her reaction to some of the composers who were soon to begin experimenting with chords and tampering with the rules of harmony.

Harmony, nevertheless, was a fascinating study for me. We learned about the construction and building blocks of music with as much interest as a veterinarian learns of the anatomy of an animal, or a builder, the framework of a house.

Rather strangely, Mr. Marriot, who wrote the harmony book, taught ear training. All but the dedicated students must have been bored out of their skulls with this class, as he never varied his procedure. Each lesson consisted of his playing a simple tune on the piano (no chords) which we were to write on our score paper. This was a piece of cake for me as I had a good ear and had no trouble even when it came to more difficult tunes like *Clare de Lune.*

My fourth class was a lecture session by none other than Felix Borowski. Mr. Borowski was a rather well-known modern composer - for which he will more likely be remembered than for his lectures. I am afraid I did not reap many rewards from that course. The class sat in a large, dark theater and he was far away on the stage, quoting facts about the history of music. We passed the course just by being there.

As with many ventures, my schooling was costing more than I had planned, and unless different financial arrangements were made I would face the possibility of returning home at the end of the semester. However, fate intervened in the form of a phone call from Ethel Lukens, who had taught music in Buffalo when I was a student, and whose mother still lived there.

Ethel was married to a man who traveled a lot and she needed help with her two small children. Here was a chance to get my room and board for free by looking after the children and helping with the housework. The latter took up practically all my spare time, but I stayed with it since it made more sense than quitting school. We got along very well, and I did have an opportunity to practice on Ethel's piano.

Ethel was a native of Buffalo where her parents owned one of the early grocery stores, "Adams and Young." Her husband, Penn Lukens, whom she met while attending school in Illinois, was a business consultant in Chicago.

I missed the girls' club and its services; I was making a 180-degree turn. My interesting conversations with the Prairie Avenue girls were replaced by the chatter of a three and a five year old, however, some of my former roommates and I met occasionally downtown for lunch.

On one such occasion I was meeting one of the girls from the club at the Peacock tea room when I literally ran into Clarence Matteson as I entered the revolving door at the entrance. Clarence, a young man from Buffalo who was starting his dentistry practice in the city, joined us for lunch. We probably bored my girlfriend to death with our gossip about Buffalo. I saw Clarence several times after that and enjoyed discussing our experiences in the big city.

One morning earlier in the year as I was leaving school to walk to my room on Prairie Avenue, I was joined by a fellow student who asked if I would mind if she walked a ways with me. I was delighted and intrigued when she asked if I was from the West. "Why," I replied, "I'm from Wyoming. How did you know?"

"Oh," she said, "No one from around here would have a tan like yours!" (Many of the girls at the club were very curious about the West, and wanted to know all about what it was really like - making me quite popular. Their previous perceptions had been rather warped from westerns that they had seen).

That was the beginning of a friendship which has lasted seven decades. Her name was Elsie Clements. She lived with her parents and brother, Hans, in a large attractive apartment on the North Side. I was invited to their place several times. These visits filled a void that I needed filled - family life.

Elsie's family had given up a cafe business in St. Louis to move to the city where they thought Elsie's talents as a pianist might be more expertly developed. Her father was also a great musician and bass singer. Mrs. Clements took care of three or four boarders, young

German men recently from Europe who were struggling through night school and working days.

Everyone in the household had heard of the romantic West through movies and other media, so were most eager to hear of the wild country from one who lived there. I suppose I may have disillusioned them as I told it the way I saw it: the cowboy as a hard-working, bashful hired hand, honest as the day is long but generally lacking in social graces. Perhaps the romantic aura he seemed to possess was the result of his free life, most of which is spent outdoors in all kinds of weather; a man who is more at ease on a horse than on a cement sidewalk. He, as well as most other residents of the West, were free from the picky irritations which plagued city folks, like noise and traffic. Most of all, I believe the trait I found most different between the city dwellers and the rural Westerner was the former's disinterest in their neighbors, as contrasted to the great compassion the entire western community feels toward one another.

Elsie's father sang in a professional quartet which performed at weddings, funerals, and other social events. The Clements Quartet occasionally appeared on the Edgewater Beach Hotel radio station WEBH. At that time, radio stations were dependent upon volunteer talent for their entertainment since very little advertising was done over the air. Mr. Clements asked Elsie and me if we would like to play the piano for the radio station sometime. I was all agog to do so, of course, so he set a date for us. The station accepted us on his recommendation.

A week or so after this found Elsie and me sitting in the resplendent dining room of the Edgewater Hotel trying not to show our lack of equanimity as we waited for our names to be called by the studio director. There, in that very same room where we sat, was Paul Whiteman and his orchestra playing dinner music. We had the privilege of meeting him later when he came into the broadcasting studio.

At last we were summoned to the sound-proof, all-glass room. I played a Rachmaninoff etude, and Elsie performed a Beethoven sonata. Following our performances, Leroy North, the director at the studio, treated us to refreshments in the dining room. During our conversation I learned Leroy had gone to school with Mark House who was, at that time, a barber and storekeeper in Kaycee, Wyoming!

I was indebted to the Clements family for many enjoyable evenings when Mr. Clements saw that Elsie and I had tickets to hear famous artists who came to town.

At the time I came to Chicago, my knowledge of classical composers and music was woefully lacking. Back home we did not own a phonograph and radio programs consisted mostly of amateur performers. Most of the music I had heard up until then we made ourselves, so it was quite an education to hear famous soloists, instrumentalists and orchestras live and in some of the most beautiful theaters in Chicago.

Earlier in the year I had an opportunity to see the operas *Carmen* and *La Traviata* with a couple of girls I knew from the club. We acted as ushers. Being the new kid, I was given a balcony area high up in the opera house. Although the performers looked teeny-tiny, the acoustics were fantastic, so we could hear the music very well, and after all, that is what we had come for.

Another facet of the city which continued to amaze me was the architecture. My previous experience with skyscrapers had been looking at small black and white illustrations in newspapers and magazines. This in no way prepared me for the awesome heights and magnificence of those department store buildings in downtown Chicago.

I loved looking at the gorgeous window displays, especially at Christmas time when each store tried to outdo the others. I would venture to say the displays in one of those huge windows cost as much as the New York Store's entire inventory in Buffalo. I liked to make the visits to these windows by myself so I could stand and dream as long as I liked.

The Wrigley Building

I had an opportunity to visit the Chicago Art Institute with Willah Burrows, an art student I had met at the club. It is one of the finest museums in Chicago and contains many fine masterpieces. I vividly remember *The Blue Boy*, on loan there at the time. From that day, those little two-by-four pictures I had studied in grade school took on a new meaning. The very size of the originals was an enlightenment to me, and to see up close the actual brush strokes of the old masters was thrilling.

Another new experience was the day Elsie and I and some of our friends went for a canoe ride on the lake. It was a new sensation, but not exactly a relaxing one for me as we floated around on the water in that fragile little craft. I felt better when my feet touched the sand of the beach.

Verna & Elsie canoeing on Lake Michigan

On another occasion we boarded a stern-wheeler and cruised to the end of the lake and back. I was a little uneasy on this excursion also. I was about as comfortable as my friends might have been riding horses across a sagebrush flat in Wyoming. Terra firma under our feet would have been equally welcome.

In looking back, I guess I developed a new understanding of why the difference in lifestyles between the city and the small town make their residents different also. When I compared the hundreds of thousands of people in a city to the three or four thousand in a town, I understood why the needs of the former were provided on such a grand scale. Such hordes of people required adequate modes of transportation - elevated railroads, buses, inter-urban trains and taxis.

Even entertainment of all kinds was provided through art galleries, libraries, museums, zoos, beautiful theaters, and sports arenas. All of these marvels of civilization were provided in a most professional manner, but something was lacking - the personal touch.

In the small rural communities, such as those in the West, such services were not provided by some unknown entity, but were provided by us for us. I believed then, as now, that people who provide for themselves on a person-to-person basis are richer in many ways than our city cousins who pay for less personal services.

At the end of the second semester, I had finished my one year course of study at the Chicago Musical College and received my diploma - a piece of sheepskin which had been signed by several deans of the college, many who went on to become famous musicians. I was ready to return home and try my hand at teaching piano.

Chapter 5

Country Schools

The Burger family continued to grow, and by the time I was in high school I had five brothers. My only sister, Marjorie, died at age six in 1916 of spinal meningitis which, at that time, was considered incurable.

My older brother was Lawrence, next after me came Melvin, then Marland (Bear), followed a few years later by Ralph and Leland. Dick, the sixth and youngest, made his appearance several years later, after I had started teaching.

With all these boys, my parents decided to move to the country. Dad acquired 310 acres of land from the state, land that had previously been a part of Fort McKinney. He bought it primarily for the excellent gravel beds which he could use in his masonry business. Part of the original place is still owned by my brother Ralph. When I was a junior in high school we built a comfortable, modern, four-bedroom house on the acreage, and after disposing of the Buffalo property, we moved to the "ranch."

This was our home for several years. The southern exposure and light, sandy soil was an excellent spot for a garden. Dad set out a large apple orchard which was producing apples in a very short time, and still is, according to the present owner. Mother loved her garden and had beautiful vegetables as well as strawberries, raspberries and rhubarb. These, along with milk and cream from our milk cow and mother's great cooking, supplied our family with a cuisine which I am sure we didn't appreciate until we were gone from home.

Burger summer ranch

One other asset of this ranch was a very cold spring a short ways from the house. There was no REA (Rural Electric Association) to supply electricity at that time, so Dad built a tight box which was set down into the spring, and here Mother kept her milk in one-half gallon lard buckets. On the lid of each bucket she placed objects to tell us which bucket to use first: a leaf for the freshest, a stick for the next, and a rock for the oldest. By the time we got to the third container, a nice layer of thick cream would have risen to the top.

We had a wall telephone - one of many on the same Klondike line. We needed to go through a central operator and each family had a different ring. Ours was one long and three short rings '_____ _ _ _'. The bell was powered by batteries in the phone box which, of course, had to be replaced periodically.

When the three younger boys were ready for school, transportation became a problem. After a couple of years of struggling with cars that wouldn't start, long walks over the hills to high school, and missed school for the little boys, our parents decided upon another move. For a few years, the family rented a house for the winter, moving back to the ranch in the summer.

By the end of the following summer, I was beginning to have mixed feelings about piano teaching. I was still young enough to be a bit adventuresome, and this vocation was curtailing my activities. Many of the children that I was teaching had to have their lessons on Saturdays, and I was ready to have my Saturdays to myself again. In addition, the "outrageous" fee that I was charging - $5.00 a month, was not always easy to collect. Many of the parents ignored the bills that I sent, even though they continued to send their children for lessons.

After weighing the pros and cons of continuing, I opted in favor of teaching school. Among the *pros* of piano teaching were the tremendous rewards of finding and watching the progress of a very talented student. I had a few of them, most of whom went on and did very well with their music. I still maintain that learning a little about music will give one a greater appreciation of all kinds of music- a lifetime benefit.

I was offered a country school near the Klondike Ranch, so my next step was to pick up a few additional hours of education in order to renew my certification. There were extension classes offered at Newcastle, so

Marsha Bandy Brock and I took advantage of them. Thus followed a most interesting and educational summer.

We were fortunate to secure room and board at the home of Rev. and Mrs. Lewis Weary, formerly of Buffalo. Mrs. Weary was a great cook, but not exactly a proponent of her husband's sermons.

While in Newcastle, Marsha and I were privileged to take some scenic trips to the Black Hills. Mr. Schwiering, father of the noted artist, Conrad Schwiering, was one of our instructors. He was quite musical and organized a male quartet for which I played. So we got a bit of culture along with academic subjects.

Upon my return to Buffalo I had a short time to prepare for another move - to my school at Klondike 15 miles south of Buffalo. I lived with the Hakerts the first half of the year; this was within a short walking distance of the schoolhouse. The first morning, I walked in and saw more than a dozen children dressed in their best and eager for the first day of school, and to size up their new teacher.

I was also eager, but at the same time a little apprehensive, as this was going to be quite a change from my former teaching experiences where I had only one or two pupils. However this year proved to be a most interesting one. I had five cute little first grade girls, all of whom were quick to learn. What a thrill it is for a teacher to watch the rapid progress of youngsters who go from merely recognizing letters to being able to read an entire story for their parents by Christmas time.

Several of my former students still live in the Buffalo area, and it is always a pleasure to see and talk to them.

Klondike students

The Hakert brothers, John, Bill and Henry, and their sister, Mary, operated the Klondike Dude Ranch. The house was a fairly new, attractive frame building with a full basement which contained a large kitchen and living quarters for Mr. and Mrs. Hakert, Sr., who did all of the cooking. The hired hands ate in a dining room adjacent to the kitchen.

A tad better fare was prepared for the guests, also by the elder Hakerts, and toted upstairs by Mary to a large, bright guest dining room. After the paying guests had gone, the rest of us joined the few remaining residents and hired hands downstairs for our meals. Only then did I get my first glimpse of the cooks - a quite large lady and her very small husband. I found them interesting and different. They were Austrians who had moved west from an Austrian settlement in Minnesota.

I often wondered if they didn't get quite lonely. I never knew of anyone who came to see them except members of their family.

Henry had a couple of horses that he had trained to do a few tricks. One horse would lie down with his saddle on, a feat he did not like to perform since the saddle didn't make a comfortable bed. He was soon convinced that lying on a saddle was less painful than the alternative. After he had taken his position, the second horse, also saddled with rider aboard, placed his front feet on the saddle. The rider would then stand in the saddle and salute the crowd with his ten-gallon hat. I took the place of the rider one day while Mary took my picture. It is a good thing the shutter was set at high speed!

Besides the paying dudes, there were a few hands who worked for their board, plus a little extra, just for the privilege of spending a summer on a Wyoming ranch. One of them was a young man, Bill Petrie, who used up a lot of 23-cent gas that winter hauling me around in his "cool" Model T Ford.

One evening my mother called to tell me my brother Bear had started out afoot to join Melvin and his friend Cliff, who were running a trap line in the vicinity of the ranch. After he left the mercury had suddenly dropped to 20 degrees or less.

Mother worried about lots of little things, but this time she had reason for concern. No one lived near the Klondike road at the time, so the upshot was that Bill saddled a couple of horses and we set out in brilliant moonlight on our mission. After about an hour ride due north following a snow-covered back road, we came to the little shack with a kerosene light burning and smoke coming out of the chimney. All was well. Bear had made it with no trouble.

They didn't seem especially surprised to see us. I think my brothers, by this time, had learned to expect the unexpected! Cliff was at the table mixing up dough for a pie - at 9:30! He didn't bother with any amenities but said, "I'm sure glad you showed up, Verna. We've been arguing for 30 minutes about whether or not you put baking powder in pie dough!"

We didn't wait for the finished product, but headed back to the ranch - a slow trip as the snow was crusted. Nevertheless, it was a beautiful trip in silence; the solitude seemed to intensify the splendor of the evening, which lives in my memory as one of nature's masterpieces. I was so glad to report to mother everything was all right. For once she was glad to hear the phone ring at 1:00 a.m.

Earlier that spring Bill Petrie had informed me he was quitting the ranch to return to Kansas and take a job in the advertising department of a newspaper there. I really had grown quite fond of Bill and hated to see him go, but at the same time I was not ready to make a definite commitment, even though I had been approached to do so. There were still places I wanted to go and things I wanted to see before I settled down. I would be losing my freedom and the privilege of making my own decisions if I committed myself.

With the beginning of warmer weather, I moved down the river about three miles to the Washbaugh Ranch, from which I rode horseback to school the rest of the year. It was a completely different atmosphere here. The Washbaughs were homey ranch folks living the kind of simple, wholesome life I remembered from my grandmother's.

The horse I rode took his own sweet time going to school, but made up for it on the return trip. I think he had in mind that bucket of oats he would have waiting for him at the barn, because the closer he got to the ranch, the faster he went. I scarcely had time to get my foot in the stirrup after closing each of the three gates when he would be off at full gallop. One day when I got off to open the second gate, a rattlesnake was stretched out near the spot where I tossed the gate down. I led my horse off a safe distance and pelted the serpent with boulders until he was securely pinned to the ground. One of the Washbaugh boys rode down and finished the job after I reported the incident.

At the close of the school year, we followed tradition by having a community picnic. These affairs were purely and simply demonstrations of everyone's gastronomic skills, served up with gusto on pie tins after which each partaker selected a spot on the ground where he sat cross-legged with his plate balanced on his shins.

I'm afraid family picnics, along with other types of community gatherings, are not as commonplace with the coming of the electronic age.

Verna in front of Yellowstone dorm, 1927

Chapter 6

A Yellowstone Savage

After school was out, it was great to get together with old schoolmates and compare notes. Due to winter weather, unimproved roads, and a dearth of transportation, we had seen very little of each other all year.

Our principle topic was finances and how we might add to our bank accounts. It was still much easier for boys to get jobs in rural areas than girls. However, we got a bit of good news one day when one of the girls, Catherine Brock, told Lois Watkins and myself that Yellowstone Park was hiring college students at the park's camps. Furthermore, Mrs. W.P. Keays knew the manager of Mammoth Camp. We forthwith sought out Mrs. Keays who told us to whom we should write. We wasted no time in getting our epistles off. Perhaps I had a slight edge when stating my abilities to help with daily entertainment because of my recent musical training. At any rate, I was the lucky one of the three.

All my life I have eagerly anticipated any change in my environment or lifestyle. I had never been to Yellowstone Park and the idea of spending an entire summer there was unbelievable. I received instructions from park personnel as to date of arrival, kind of clothing and other items I would need, and was advised what route to take. As I rode on that chugging train from Sheridan to Gardiner, Montana I didn't mind it a bit. I thought I was floating along on Cloud Nine.

We were met by a park conveyance which took us to Mammoth Hot Springs. This was an unpretentious place composed of a large frame building which housed the dining room and kitchen, staff offices, and off one side, the laundry. Dotting the hillside were simple one-room cabins with no running water. Each room contained beds, washstands and portable commodes. These rooms were for the guests.

Not far from the main building were several very plain cabins of four rooms, each room housing two park workers. The only convenience any of us had was a single electric light bulb hanging from the ceiling.

Our first evening there was spent at the assembly hall where the head manager, Miss Hiwinkle, or "Lady Hi", as we called her, briefed us on our duties and the rules of the camp. We were governed by the same regulations as were found in many college dormitories.

The waitresses, or "heavers", of which I was one, attended a couple of sessions with the head waitress and her assistant, who were also hostesses. They taught us the fine points of waiting tables. To this day, I am conscious of the very few waitresses I have encountered who follow the correct etiquette of serving. As we began our duties the next morning, I met boys and girls from all over the United States, but I was the lone Wyomingite.

Lady Hi was loved and respected. I know of no serious infractions during the summer, at least none that were brought to the attention of Lady Hi!

My assigned roommate was a girl from Greenfield, Iowa named Marie. She was cute as a button, and we felt we had a special bond when we discovered that her dad and my dad's brother, George Burger, worked together at the same flour mill. Marie was engaged to a boy back home in Iowa and remained staunchly true to him all summer.

The gorgeous scenery and relaxed atmosphere of the Park had a positive effect on all of us. The colorful terraces of travertine continuously overflowing with hot springs, the towering mountains nearby, the docile-appearing buffalo in the nearby pasture, all combined to create a sense of euphoria. Remember, these were the days before radio and television. No piped-in music greeted the guests as they embarked from their old-fashioned motor coaches and entered the lounge. Nevertheless, they were not without a welcome. All of us who could were right there on the verandah with our ukuleles playing and singing our hearts out.

The young folks who worked at the Park were called "savages" and were further categorized as "heavers" (waitresses), "pillow punchers" (cabin girls), "bubble queens" (laundry girls), "pack rats" (bus boys), and "cabin porters". The bus boys carried the heavy trays for the heavers, and the cabin porters carried the heavy stacks of linen for the pillow punchers. One of their less glamorous duties was to "shoot the ducks," translated: take care of the portable commodes.

With such beautiful surroundings, idyllic atmosphere and camaraderie provided by the boys and girls working and entertaining together, a few romances were inevitable. The pack rat from Notre Dame eventually married the pillow puncher from Northwestern. One of our fellow heavers married an older man soon after the park season closed. Another girl, who fell madly in love with a man about town from

California, never heard from him again after she went back to school. Many other less serious couples just simply enjoyed the camaraderie of fellow workers.

Hardly anyone had a car, but many interesting points could be reached on foot. It was considered a "large" evening to wheedle the pantry man out of material for sandwiches and other goodies, then hike up to Mount Washburn on moonlit nights and enjoy a midnight supper around a campfire. I shudder to think what might happen if such freedoms were allowed today in these hallowed park grounds.

I dated a Park Ranger named Ray most of the summer. He lived in Gardiner, where I met his delightful mother. She let me know Ray was an only child and since she had no daughter to plan for, showed me a drawer full of linens she had embroidered for her son's future use. Wow! I was beginning to feel a little bit like the fly in the spider's parlor! Ray had his own car which was considered a real bonus. We made a couple of trips around the loop. He knew every inch of the Park and was a great guide.

I became acquainted with Ruth and Estaline Howrey, two sisters from Iowa who were attending the music school at Northwestern University in the fall. They begged me to return to Chicago and enroll with them. It was a great temptation as I had saved all my tips that summer and most of my wages. I told Ruth and Estaline that I would go home and think it over.

My brother Melvin had bought a brand new Ford roadster that summer and had written me he would like to visit the Park and take me back to Buffalo. That sounded like more fun than the train, as well as more convenient and cheaper.

Hot springs in Yellowstone Park

He drove into camp the day before we left and was welcomed to the farewell festivities that pretty well took up the last couple of days before we said our last sad goodbyes to our many summer friends and departed for our various destinations. My last goodbye with Ray included a proposal of marriage which rather took me by surprise.

I told him so, and promised to give it serious consideration.

Melvin and I had a wonderful scenic trip home which I enjoyed as much as he did, since all the scenery through the Big Horn Basin and from Ten Sleep to Buffalo was new to me also. It took a few days to relate my experiences to my interested parents and to all my friends, who were probably not that interested. If my betters expressed any doubts as to the wisdom of spending another year in Chicago on a shoe string, I didn't listen, and in a matter of days I was on my way again. This time I was a more seasoned traveler with assurance that I would be met by friends who would get me through the necessary steps to once again get settled in the city.

Before I conclude this chapter, I feel I must digress a bit and bring the reader up to date regarding Bill, my Klondike country beau and Ray, my Yellowstone Park Romeo. Bill was a faithful long-distance suitor all summer. For awhile I got a letter a day and two on Monday (at three cents a piece!). I tried to keep my replies as casual as my feelings for him were, and gradually his familiar envelopes became fewer and fewer until they ceased all together, sometime after I returned to the city.

As to Ray and his proposal, without that romantic setting, beautiful scenery and utterly carefree living, the magic seemed to be gone. I hoped Ray was experiencing the same reaction after returning to more normal living conditions. I guess the feeling was mutual. We exchanged a few polite letters, but after these ceased I didn't hear from him again until 1933, when he came to Buffalo and made some inquiries as to my whereabouts. I was married by that time.

Romance seemed to move further and further away into the future as I settled down to more mundane duties and preparations that would affect my more immediate future. I had less than two weeks to make final arrangements if I intended entering the fall term at the University. Correspondence was sent and received. I was notified that I was accepted at the music school at Northwestern and assigned a room at a private home, since all the dorms were full at that date.

Just two years had passed from the time I had first boarded that train on my first big adventure, and now I was off again! This time with not so much a feeling of wonder, as a feeling of great anticipation. This time I had some idea of what I would experience and of the many wonderful things I had seen and might explore further.

After a rather uneventful trip (no fairy godmother this time), I finally heard the clang of the engine's bell signifying that we had reached our destination. We didn't stop at Union Station this time, but at a smaller depot in Evanston. Here I was met by Ruth Howrey, my Yellowstone Park friend. She went with me to my new abode, the home of Judge and Mrs. Warner, where I was to share a room with Elsa Lowenstein, a vocal major in the school of music.

After unpacking the essentials, I went off with Ruth to her little apartment where we had a bite of supper with her sister, Estaline. After a delightful evening, during which we tried to relate all that had happened since we saw each other, I went back to my room which was not far away. It was time to get some rest before making my appearance as a student at the prestigious Northwestern University.

Chapter 7

Return to Chicago

Since the day I walked onto the campus of Northwestern University in Evanston, Illinois in 1926, I have had the privilege of visiting several college campuses, including the University of Wyoming at Laramie, University of Washington at Seattle, SMU at Dallas, Texas A & M College Station, and the University of Colorado at Boulder. They all have their own particular personalities portrayed by architecture and grounds.

Northwestern's buildings were mostly red stone of matching style. The landscaping followed the rather severe lines of the structures. In fact, when I went through the entrance of that tall steel fence which surrounded the entire campus for the first time and beheld the institution as a whole, the following adjectives would probably have described my impressions: stern, massive, serious, awesome, and above all, no nonsense. At each entrance were signs designating the campus as a "no smoking" area. I have since wondered how long those signs remained there and now I wonder how long before they will be put back!

The music school occupied a relatively small area along the western border of the campus. That is where I took myself that cool September morning, with my transcripts in hand and a bit of trepidation in my heart as I approached the desk of the registrar. However, we soon had things in order, and my next step was to buy supplies. I made good use of the second hand book store, getting most of what I needed for orchestration, public school, music and English literature. My assignments for voice and piano would come later. It was also necessary to receive some orientation at this time so I wouldn't blunder around too much trying to find my classrooms when I came back the next morning.

At last I was ready to return to my room at the Warner's. I really hadn't had time to take a good look at it. It was a Victorian edifice, three stories high, furnished on the first floor with Victorian furniture, and presided over by a Victorian couple, Judge and Mrs. Warner.

Elsa and I had a room on the third floor. It was furnished a tad better than a monk's cell. Our beds were narrow cots and far from soft. Elsa had brought an extra pad to put on hers, but I endured mine the way it was. Mrs. Warner had advised us against cooking in our rooms. However, we had a little Sterno stove and felt the need to save a few pennies now and then by making a little toast and heating up a can of soup for lunch. I think Mrs. Warner had the nose of a bloodhound, for as soon as our toast or soup was about ready we could hear the "creak, creak" on the first flight of stairs. However, it was no problem to get all the evidence put away and be hard at work at our study table by the time she got to our door.

Elsa was also running on a tight budget, so we were always looking for bargains where we could save a couple of nickels. We found a little restaurant nearby where we could get a dish of oatmeal and a piece of toast for 15 cents. I think sometimes we varied our menu a bit on Sundays, but we got by on that monotonous meal all year. We even cut out coffee since it didn't supply any nourishment.

Ruth came by in a few days to visit. She had been working occasionally in a small lunch room not far from campus. She said they were having a special luncheon on Friday and needed extra help. I was delighted to put in

Boarding house, Chicago

for the job as it meant tips and a free meal. Perhaps my training the previous summer at Yellowstone Park proved to be an asset. At any rate, Miss Parr, the proprietor, hired me, and after the luncheon was over she asked if I could come back on Monday. In a short time I was on the regular staff, along with Thaddeus Elisor of Birmingham, Alabama, a student at the nearby Garrett Bible Institute.

I hadn't intended for it to work out that way, but Ruth's part time job became my full time job for the rest of the year. Ruth didn't hold this against me, as she really didn't want to work and besides, a wealthy Iowa farmer uncle was subsidizing both her and her sister.

Miss Parr's lunch room was an attractive little place owned and operated by three elderly but efficient spinsters. They lived together in a large, old-fashioned house, where once a week a group of Evanston doctors and medical experts met for a business lunch in the big dining room. I was moved from the Lunch Room to this location on these occasions. This was different, to be sure. Their conversation during lunch was a bit unnerving until I learned to turn a deaf ear on their candid and detailed discussions of such things as Mr. Bigby's liver or Mrs. Kettle's intestines.

The Lunch Room catered mostly to members of the University faculty plus a few business and professional men from around town, most of whom came back every day. Thad and I thus became well-acquainted with many of them, including a dark-haired, handsome young jazz piano player. I was thrilled when he had time to talk music with me for a short time. Another one was a not-so-young book dealer who gave Thad and me books which he autographed. And then there was the lawyer who offered me a part time job in his office. (More about him later).

The cook was a big, rawboned Irish girl who wore her heart on her sleeve and willingly shared her sentiments with everyone. She was married to a sailor who, it appeared from his long absence, was beginning to prefer the girls in other ports. This state of affairs affected her attitude but not her abilities to fulfill her duties as cook. She was indeed a master in the kitchen, as was evidence by her faithful clientele.

Jennie, the wizened little woman who did the scrubbing on her hands and knees, swore allegiance to me for life because I stopped to inquire about her health and said a few kind words to her once in awhile. All she ever heard from Miss Parr and others were orders. Jennie had lost a brother in Casper, Wyoming in the early '20's and had sent some money to the coroner to pay for his burial, but had heard nothing. At her request I wrote the county coroner to see if a record might be had, but I had no more luck than she had. At the time of his death, considering the rather untamed conditions in the early Wyoming oil fields, it probably would not have been wise to pursue it. Anyway, I tried to console poor Jennie by saying that most likely everything was properly taken care of.

Thad and I became good pals as we worked together. He was working toward his doctorate in theology and had a keen mind. We spent many Sunday afternoons at our favorite drug store, not far from my place, munching on olive and nut sandwiches while we discussed everything under the sun.

One afternoon I decided to take the lawyer up on his offer. I could use every penny I could earn. When Thad learned I was going to the office, he insisted on accompanying me and stayed until I went home. After a couple of afternoons of this, I put two and two together and didn't go back. The job I was given was absolutely inane. Thad had read that man's character which he thought might come to the fore when left alone with an unsophisticated gal from Wyoming. That was the end of my "legal secretary" experience.

There was a bulletin at school where jobs wanted and jobs available were listed. I left a note saying I needed most any kind of work (except working for lascivious lawyers, a reservation in my mind only). In a day or two I had a call from a lady in exclusive north Evanston wanting me to babysit. I got in touch with her and was to arrive at her place at 7:45 p.m. on Friday.

After vaguely charting my route on our Chicago map, I started out Friday evening to my first babysitting job. It was "a 'fur' piece" indeed. It took me longer to walk there than anticipated, so I was a bit late. The parents met me at the door all dressed to go out. The father was a handsome man, whom I learned was a doctor when he handed me a telephone number to call in case of an emergency. The mother was a stunning young woman who barely had time to tell me her daughters' names before she and her husband were off to their gala evening, leaving me in charge of the house and two darling little girls. I knew no more about them than they did me, but we fared very well and thus began a job which lasted the rest of the year. In fact, the family wanted me to move in with them, but I didn't want to give up my freedom or my interesting job at the Lunch Room, so I declined.

During my second year in Chicago, I saw quite a bit of the Clements who were my "second family" that first year. My good friend, Elsie, had married Albert Lukas. He had a great business going in connection with Bausch and Lomb Optical. Albert had become an expert in repairing and installing microscopes, so he was in demand at the University and at other laboratories all over.

I spent Thanksgiving with them, and we attended a few functions downtown, but mostly what I liked best about them was that they provided me a touch of family life which I longed for most of all.

At Christmas time I was invited to Eaton, Indiana, to the home of the George Hoovers. Their daughter,

Arliss, a distant cousin of mine, had visited in Wyoming several summers. I rode down on the train and had a most enjoyable week at their lovely home. We visited Muncie, Indiana where another daughter lived and where we visited Ball College. We drove to Indianapolis where we peeked through the cracks of the board fence that surrounded the Indy Race Track. That was as close as I ever got to the Indy 500.

By the middle of the year, I decided I couldn't afford another term at the musical college so I transferred to the college of liberal arts, which was about half the cost of the specialized school. That was a real challenge but I loved it. If I would have had the money, I think I probably would have continued majoring in Political Science or Geography. As it was, I started making plans to return to Wyoming in June. My family had written that my mother was ailing and might have to have an operation in August. It seemed my place was most likely there in Buffalo to sort of fill the gap while she was gone.

With very little added expense, I found I could go home via Oregon, Missouri and visit my grandparents, Ulrich and Christina Burger. They were both getting old, and Grandfather was nearly blind. I took the train to Mound City and was driven over to Oregon by a friend of the family. My two weeks there were so rewarding. Grandfather loved to have me read to him, and Grandmother was delighted to have someone to talk about family with.

There was a grown daughter living with them who had Down's syndrome. At that time there were no special schools available or no special education, so she had grown up with meager training provided only by Grandmother. While I was there I taught her to do simple running stitch fancywork. She was as proud of her simple accomplishment as if it had been a masterpiece of art. Their youngest son Ted, who was just my age, being the last of nine children, also lived at home and worked for the highway department. He took me and Lucille, the girl who helped with the housework, on several expeditions.

Ted was no different than young folks of today. He invested his wages in a new Ford. The three of us drove to Mound City to pick up a friend of Lucille's who was to come in on the midnight interurban. She was not aboard, so we departed for home. The hour was late, Ted had worked all day, so the inevitable happened - he went to sleep. We drove off into a barbed wire fence. The impact threw us out into a bed of tall grass, with no injuries except to me. I hit the fence, cutting a three-inch gash in my knee. Ted managed to get the car on the road, a crushed fender the only damage.

My clothes were in a pretty gory state by the time we got home. What a shock it must have been for Grandmother when the three of us walked in. She called the family doctor who dressed and met us at his office. I squeezed Ted's hand while the doctor sewed up the cut with a huge needle and thread that looked as big as fish line, all sans anesthetic!

Chapter 8

Marriage

During the summer of 1926, I served as Mother's right hand while she was incapacitated during and following surgery in the Sheridan hospital.

It was a busy summer, but I thoroughly enjoyed my new tasks of housekeeping. I could at least see the results of my labors and learned a great deal about cooking, as Mother wasn't there all the time to tell me what to do next.

My father was busy with his cement work. Two or three of my brothers were helping him and stayed at home. Also, one or two other boys who were working during vacation found it convenient to board at our house. I had seven or eight people for most meals. We were living in the High Street house, and it had a large kitchen which Dad had remodeled to make it a very convenient place to prepare meals and serve many people.

I managed to give a few piano lessons during my spare time, mostly to adults who had not had an opportunity earlier in their lives. My youngest brother Dick was five and started to kindergarten that fall. It took some planning to get breakfast for the workers then have Dick cleaned up, fed, and off to school thirty minutes later.

All of that was valuable experience as I learned to schedule my time, a practice I have pretty much adhered to ever since.

During that winter I was a substitute pianist at the Bison Theatre, playing for the silent movies. We would be issued a cue sheet a day ahead which suggested music to play for each scene, whether deeply romantic or dangerously active. We really didn't get to watch all the movie as our attention was divided between the cue sheet and the music in front of us. However, after two shows a night for two or three nights, we found we could give quite an accurate review of the movie.

One winter a vaudeville show came to town. Their piano player had become ill so the Chamber of Commerce secretary called to see if I could fill the spot. I went down for rehearsal and found the music quite simple. In fact, the entire cast was quite simple! I played for the troupe. They offered me a job if I would accompany them on their tour. Wow! That sounded about as appealing as selling artificial flowers on street corners - to listen to those jokes just once was more than enough!

I believe it was the American Legion who later that year put on a variety show which was directed by a professional who traveled around the country putting on shows. It was very interesting to see how she selected her cast. There was a terrific turn-out by girls and boys who wanted to try their abilities as performers. There was absolutely no favoritism shown in this lady's selections. She picked her cast entirely on their abilities and talents, not because of their families and/or connections. As a consequence, the cast consisted of some who had never had the opportunity to do a solo part on stage before, even though they would have liked to. The show was a fantastic success and received great audience reaction. I played for all the singing and dance numbers which was so gratifying, as the participants so thoroughly enjoyed performing.

Tony Preston, who worked at the local land office in Buffalo, was an excellent trumpet player and organized a band of six members. Most of us played by note, so Tony ordered orchestrations for us to follow, which we did with no original embellishments. This was in contrast to another group of musicians with which a couple of my brothers played. They played by ear, as did most of their band, so their music was much more spontaneous and most likely had better rhythm. Anyway, they got more jobs than we did. We probably would have been well-suited to play dinner music in a restaurant of some sort. However, we enjoyed our practice sessions and made good music to listen to. A couple of the members I recall were Jim Gurney and Rollie Kirkland.

In the summer of 1928, I decided I needed a change of scenery and occupation. I had an interview with Frank Horton and got a job as entertainer and waitress at the HF Bar Dude Ranch. There were a couple of others working there who played drums and saxophone, respectively, so we had a passable band with which to entertain the dudes at the clubhouse.

Besides being available for music, I also helped the salad maker. She was an ex-alcoholic trying to rehabilitate herself away from town and temptation. She gave every salad a gender and a name and treated it as if it were her own creation of art - and some of them were. She was just one of the many characters I got to know that summer.

Others were the chef who kept his liquor in the coffeepot, and the mechanic who kept the light plant going, but was equally capable of causing a blackout right in the middle of a party.

I stayed on the ranch until the middle of September. After most of the guests left and the college help went off to school, the rest of us closed the summer operations, readying the cabins, water pipes, yards, tack rooms, etc., for the winter.

There was a real air of camaraderie among those who were left. We entertained ourselves with music, cookouts, or whatever we liked, so it was with reluctance I left for Buffalo to see about starting up my piano lessons again.

I traded in my old upright piano and purchased a Wurlitzer studio grand which I proudly displayed in my music room at High Street. My students included a banker's wife, a landman's wife, a filling station attendant, a few high school boys who wanted to play jazz, and children of all ages.

Music room at High Street house

I remember one mother who thought all it took to make her rather slow, normal son a musician was the fact that his aunt could play. Another father thought it worked sort of like a machine where you put in a nickel and got something in return. He thought that as long as he gave me a check every month, his daughter would, without question, soon become a musician.

There were several in the class, however, who really made a most credible showing at our spring recital. All the mothers showed up and I'm sure they all marveled inwardly at the accomplishments of their offspring.

The winter provided the usual diversions for young people - mostly country dances or town dances at the old City Hall.

I taught a Sunday School class of fifth and sixth graders who were more enthusiastic than one can imagine. They loved having parties and entertaining their parents. I continued to play at the movies occasionally, as talkies were not to appear in Buffalo for some time yet.

The following summer I returned to the dude ranch. This summer I was in charge of a private dining room which seated two or three children, each with an individual governess. Two of the youngsters I vaguely remember as being normal and well-behaved, but one I do remember well, and often wonder what became of him. His governess was a cranky old lady who knew nothing of children, especially a child who was a high strung five-year-old needing special understanding and love, none of which he got from his nanny or from his parents.

His mother was a beautiful but shallow young woman, and his father was an aging white-haired man who probably had learned the hard way that beauty is only skin deep. They seldom visited the dining room, but on those rare occasions that they did they must have noticed that the little fellow and I had developed a pretty good rapport by the end of the season. The parents came to me a week or so before they were to leave and asked me if I would consider accompanying them back to New York as a governess. After thinking it over, I found more cons than pros, prompting me to decline. Although this little guy could have had anything he wanted materially, he didn't get what he needed most - love and concern from those around him. He was fast developing into a revengeful and antagonistic child. He could hardly be blamed entirely if, in his adult life, he turned out to be a useless if not detrimental citizen.

This second summer, the year being 1929, our orchestra consisted of an excellent saxophone player, Bob Jones, and Jay Cristler who was great in the percussion section. I was at the piano. I think we sounded pretty good, and we had a good "beat" which, after all, is all those dudes needed. Once in a while, the guests would find themselves with nothing to do in the evening, and since very few of them seemed to enjoy their own company, would come tapping at my door with a polite request for a little piano music. So off to the club house we would go.

One weekend I had a date for a dance in Buffalo. One of my old high school friends was there with her husband, Art. Art asked me if I had met Sandy out at the HF Bar Ranch. I hadn't, but it appeared I was about to as Art had just seen him downtown. He went down and came back with a tall, interesting-looking stranger who wasn't a stranger very long, as he wanted every dance. Sandy, I soon learned, was manager of Paradise Ranch, also owned by the HF Bar. He spent lots of time at the main ranch, and we had a most enjoyable summer. We made a few trips up to Paradise which they planned to open for guests the next season.

One day when we drove there, we discovered a lady sitting on the porch all by herself. She was a rancher's wife from the Kaycee country and said she had come up there to "think things over." I gathered she had a few interests outside her domestic realm and was trying to decide what to do about them. Sandy filled me in later - I was right - she evidently had more than a mere speaking acquaintance with some of the guests that summer.

Prohibition was still in effect, but the guests had their sources. This situation, plus the absolutely carefree atmosphere of the ranch, inevitably led to a few affairs. However, if they involved anyone locally it could have been a bit unsettling to them, because when the season was over the guests went back to their own world and business, leaving the locals to get back to their own lifestyles, which probably seemed a little drab after a whirlwind summer. Of course, it was out of sight, out of mind with their temporary friends.

One of the wranglers at the ranch was on the local school board. He approached me late in the summer with an offer of a teaching job at the HF Bar school, just a few miles down the road from the main ranch. I thought a guaranteed $110 a month sounded pretty nice, so I decided to take the job. I spent a week in Buffalo getting things ready, then went back to the ranch where I was to stay until it closed. By this time there were just a few paying guests left. The guests and I all had rooms in the big main building above the dining room. I rode horseback to school until sometime in November. In the meantime, I had discovered a small cabin a quarter mile from the school which I thought could be made livable with a little work.

Mr. Horton gave me permission to use the cabin, and told me to help myself to any furnishing I needed from the ranch store room. My dad came out and mended the floor, chinked the logs, and whitewashed the entire structure inside. I had a small campstove and a pot-bellied heating stove which, along with the other necessities supplied by the HF Bar, kept me quite cozy.

The cabin was across the creek from the school house so I purchased some lightweight boots which I wore to school, then changed to other shoes. I had thirteen or fourteen kids in school, all of whom rode horseback to and from their homes. I had a couple of high school girls who gave me no trouble except when it came to Latin. I had no translation for the book we were using.

I was still seeing Sandy Jacques and when I mentioned my dilemma to him, he took me to meet his sister, Vera, who had just arrived from Boston where she taught Latin in a girls' school. She took my book and went through the entire text with me, writing the translation. I am sure I learned more in that evening than in nine months of high school, with the added bonus of making a new and enjoyable friend, Vera Jacques.

By November all of the guests were gone and the ranch was closed up. Sandy had gone to California to manage a resort at Carmel. We exchanged a few letters, but I was so busy with school and weekend activities that our correspondence finally petered out. Sandy was a Columbia University alumni, but never had acquired the knack of writing letters. His letters proved to be a poor substitute for his vivacious personality.

My neighbors, a half mile west of my teacherage were so good to me. I spent several happy evenings at the Searcy's place enjoying their simple but sincere hospitality. We had a great time playing pinochle, joined by her brother, Woodston.

Mr. Searcy kept me in chopped wood all winter and Dad brought out some coal for my heating stove. In the middle of the winter the river froze over which made getting to and from school much easier, but in the spring high water forced me to detour around an extra half mile and cross the Rock Creek bridge.

This Rock Creek school was my fifth year of teaching at rural schools, and I enjoyed it very much. I had about every grade, but we managed to make pretty good progress. However, I looked forward to weekends when someone could take me to Buffalo where I could be comfortable for awhile in my parents' home on High Street with its convenient bathroom, electricity, phone, and warmth.

I still didn't have a car - I had held off car salesmen for eight years, for I was reluctant to spend all of my money on one. I was able to get most places I wanted to go using other means, anyway.

During Christmas vacation my brothers Lawrence, Melvin, and Bear were to play at a dance at the Klondike Ranch. They wanted me to go; I wasn't too excited about it, but finally rode out with them. Lawrence had a pretty nice car at that time. There was a big crowd at the dance, including several girls from Buffalo I hadn't expected to see, and, I might add, several boys I hadn't expected to see. One of them (the best looking one there!), was Frank Davis from Sussex. We spent most of the evening together, and at the end of the dance he apologized for not being able to take me home, as he had come out with a car load of guys. I think my head was in the clouds all the way home that night.

In the weeks following the dance, I had several letters from Frank, who proved to be an excellent correspondent. I struggled over the answers laboriously, as I certainly wanted to keep those epistles coming. I guess I didn't disappoint him too much, for in a couple of weeks I was surprised one evening to hear a car drive up the road toward my cabin. It was Frank. He had just purchased a brand new Ford Model A truck which I am sure was properly initiated to the rugged life of the West when it had to ford Rock Creek in mid-winter. We went into Buffalo for the weekend, and that was just one of many weekends we did so. Before long I was counting the days from Monday to Saturday when I would hear that familiar chug of the Ford motor coming up the road, still dripping from its bath in the river. The drips would soon become icicles by the time we were ready for the return trip.

One weekend towards spring Frank met me at the school house on Friday afternoon. We had planned this earlier, and I was prepared to go on to town that afternoon. After stopping at home for a few needed articles, we went on to the Spectacle Ranch, or more properly the Turkey Track Ranch, which was Frank's brand and what he now called the former Hard Winter Davis spread.

I liked the good-sized ranch house that had been built by Mother Davis on the school section across from the original Davis place after the death of her husband, Henry (Hard Winter) Davis.

That was one of three weekends that I spent at the ranch that spring. The other trips were made with my brothers who were playing at a Sussex dance, and with a couple of hired hands from the nearby Meike Ranch. During one of these visits Frank and I made a most important decision. We decided to slip off to Sheridan and get married.

It was my choice whether or not to have a wedding. Although at this time weddings were not the lavish affairs that they are today, I still didn't think my folks had the wherewithal to finance a church wedding. Besides, the entire country was in rather bad shape economically and everyone was leaning towards the practical rather than the extravagant. If Mother ever thought differently about a wedding she never mentioned it.

Anyway, on a beautiful 29th day of March 1930, we drove over to Sheridan with my brother Bear. I went to the New York Store, bought a dress, and then we were off to the Methodist Church. There Dr. Wood, whom I liked very much as he had held services in Buffalo, tied the knot.

We postponed our honeymoon as I had six more weeks of school left. Those final weeks of school I had occasion to spend time with the families of some of my students, and then at the end of the year the patrons decided to have a farewell dance for us before I moved. Anyone who danced with the schoolmarm pinned a dollar bill on my blouse. We were able to buy a wedding gift with the proceeds of the evening.

After a few days at home gathering up my belongings, I departed for my new home with my new husband, not in a white chariot, but in a serviceable Model A Ford truck loaded with coal.

Chapter 9

The Ranch on Powder River

It was a beautiful spring day in 1930 when the newly married Mr. and Mrs. Frank Davis left Kaycee and drove down the wide, fertile Powder River Valley towards the Davis ranch.

The river meanders along at a leisurely pace, a very crooked stream bordered by wide sand bars and lined with huge cottonwood trees. A scenic pine ridge can be seen along the entire route on the south side of the river (this ridge stretches for miles - all the way to the Yellowstone River in Montana). The scene had an aura of peace and contentment. The houses, though modest, were well kept. Many trees had been planted and there were nice yards and fences. The entire area bespoke of the pride of the ranch families and their confidence in the future.

By the time we got to our mailbox and started down the mile long lane, I was tremendously excited and ready to tackle my new role, the most important "first" of my life. We chugged into the Davis ranch, threw the

suitcases off at the back door, then unloaded the coal at the coal house.

I had a sudden feeling that this could be a symbol of the priorities of ranch living - a load of coal instead of a new refrigerator or bedroom suite. I was not far off... For years we classified our purchases in three categories: Needs, Wants and Wishes. We seldom got past the first.

Frank and Verna at the Ranch, 1930

The house we moved into was a fairly new log house, built by Mother Davis after the original ranch was lost through foreclosure. She did not like living there, however, so she had bought a house in Buffalo.

Henry Winter Davis, Frank's father, came to Wyoming in 1878 to see for himself the possibilities of running cattle in the territory. At the time he was a medical student in Philadelphia, but was bitten by the bug of adventure. After familiarizing himself with the business at the ranch of his cousin, Joseph Carey (later governor of Wyoming), he and a companion traveled extensively on horseback throughout Wyoming, Idaho and Montana.

In a glowing letter to his parents, he wrote about the Powder River country, "This is wonderful cattle country, miles and miles of open range, no fences, water and feed abundant."

He acquired land on the Powder River a few miles east of what is now the town of Kaycee. Through the next several years the ranch prospered and grew until a severe blizzard in the winter of 1889 devastated the Davis herd. Davis acquired the sobriquet of "Hard Winter" and persevered until the mid-20's, when a series of reversals spelled the end of the Davis Spectacle Ranch as a large spread.

When the Homestead Act was enacted, some far-sighted legislator was responsible for reserving two sections, numbers 16 and 36, out of each township (which consists of 36 sections) to be designated as school sections. The money derived from their use was to benefit the schools. The home that Frank's mother built after leaving the Spectacle Ranch was built on a school section that had been retained by the Davis family when the rest of the land was turned over. We divided our time between that house and the log cabin on Frank's homestead during the 11 years we lived on Powder River.

Although the ranch house on the school section still contained plenty of furniture, linen, dishes, cooking utensils and other necessities to set up housekeeping, I always had the feeling that I was borrowing someone else's things. This somehow made it difficult for me to realize that this was really *our* place.

At the same time, I soon realized how fortunate we were to be supplied with all of these housekeeping items. The cattle business being what it was made it necessary to channel what money we had back into the ranch.

Frank had "bached" here for several years, and any items that he didn't use on a daily basis were stored away. The house contained only the bare necessities for everyday living. I found that by adding a feminine touch - a bedspread, a few doilies here and there, a centerpiece on the table, and by washing and starching all the ruffled curtains that hung at the many windows - I soon had the place looking like a home.

One evening after we had finished dinner Frank said, "Do you feel like a little hike this evening? I want you to meet our next door neighbors." I have always enjoyed people, but from where I sat the prospects of satisfying my gregarious instincts seemed rather dim with Frank being away hours every day. A ranch is not like an office where everything is neatly confined within four walls. A rancher has miles to cover - checking the condition of fences, location of cows, abundance of grass, availability of water, or any other aspect of the business. So I was eager to meet these neighbors that my husband apparently liked so much.

When we stepped into their cheery kitchen and Merriam and Arley Taylor came to greet us, I couldn't have received a warmer welcome from a long lost relative. What a wonderful couple - we remained friends for years after we left the ranch. After they moved to Buffalo I continued to visit them, and our mundane conversations devoid of any furbelows were so rewarding.

We lived in this school section house for several months. In the meantime, Frank was tearing down a log cabin on the old Hard Winter Davis Spectacle Ranch that had belonged to his sister, Dolly Tisdale. He marked the logs as he took them down, hauled them up the river about three miles from where we were living to his homestead site, put the logs up according to the numbers and *presto!* - we had another home.

We had lots to do before it was livable. We hired an elderly man from Buffalo to come down and frame doors, windows, and finish up the project. My dad came down and made a nice concrete floor for the back porch.

Although we lived there for several years, I continued to have that feeling of impermanence, as we never finished the cabin. We had a covered front porch with a floor of sand. It remained there as long as we did, awaiting, but never receiving, a top of concrete. No kids in the neighborhood had a bigger sand box!

Frank had a well drilling outfit which he set up on a small hill next to the house and attempted to drill a water well. This was unsuccessful so our water supply came from barrels hauled on a drag from Powder River.

The water was hard enough to "float a nail" and required a good dose of lye to get it in condition for laundry. When a white foam formed on the top I skimmed it off and my wash water would be ready. The only equipment available was a wash tub, a washboard, a rinse tub and a clothesline. Mother Davis had used the same method for the fifty years she was on the ranch, and I thought nothing of continuing.

A neighbor from across the river who had lived in similar circumstances put it this way, "First we would take a bath, then use the bath water to wash the underwear, scrub the floor, and finally water the plants!" Our drinking water was hauled from a ranch several miles north of us.

As soon as our two-room log cabin was made livable, we packed necessary items and moved up the road and across the river to our very own land and house.

In the front room were two pairs of windows that swung open to the inside. These were wonderful in the summer as they let in the maximum amount of air. The only disadvantage, as far as I could see, was that the curtains must be attached to the window itself and not to the frame; they could not be longer than the window for the same reason. A bed, a wardrobe (a four-foot shelf with a curtain), a chest of drawers, a rocking chair, and a large trunk furnished the front room.

The only other room was the kitchen, which had windows on the north, west and south. I had great fun making curtains for all of them. We were faithful customers of Montgomery Ward - I sent for a bundle of random choice remnants for 10¢ a yard. What a challenge to decide what each piece was to be used for.

We did have a sheep wagon which could accommodate overnight visitors who were brave enough to expose their car to the rigors of crossing the river.

We brought a small bookcase from the Davis Ranch which was crammed full of books, including many classics. Both of us were avid readers and supplemented our reading material by taking *The Saturday Evening Post, Cosmopolitan, Literary Digest* and *National Geographic*. How sad that we never saved the Norman Rockwell covers from *The Saturday Evening Post*!

Frank and I would discuss faraway places described in *National Geographic* magazines and dream about traveling there. We didn't get much further than those plans, but enjoyed the ideas and kept our horizons broadened beyond the sagebrush- covered hills.

Frank had an avid interest in geology and mining. Books on those subjects stood him in good stead in the later years on the mountains, and in passing that enthusiasm along to our son Jim who made it his profession.

At one end of the kitchen we placed a cot on which were piled all of our extra quilts, making a fairly comfortable couch. We covered it with a richly colored chenille door hanging or portiere, resurrected from the old Davis house. Our dining table was a homemade affair - pretty rough - but it was graced with a gaily colored oilcloth. Most everyone used that type of table covering, a predecessor to vinyl, and the variety of artistic patterns was one of the exciting choices I had about once a year when replacement was necessary.

The Davis Homestead on Powder River

The homestead was located at the foot of sagebrush-covered hills on the south bank of the Powder River. A few scraggy junipers "graced" the higher hills to the south. We were quite close to the river, which was lined with huge old cottonwoods that provided beautiful color for many months of the year. The new green leaves in the spring, the luscious foliage of the summer, followed by the brilliant fall colors gave us a feeling of tranquillity. The soft sound of the lazy river and the birds and breezes in the trees provided a perfect background for the visual effects.

Distant views from the homestead house were limited by the surrounding hills. The only view of the Big Horn Mountains could be had as we traveled west up the Sussex Road toward Kaycee.

Good neighbors meant a lot to us in this isolated location, especially Reece and Lucille Gibbs and the Bodan family. Our only close neighbors (meaning less than two miles away), they did much to relieve the monotony of our generally uneventful life. Hial and Mamie Streeter lived in a dugout cabin about three miles up the river.

These dugouts were not uncommon in the early ranch days, though most of them were very simple and used mostly for the cowboys' line camps. As you might gather from the name, a dugout consisted primarily of a hole dug back into a hill with a log front which contained the only windows. Contrary to expectations, when entering the Streeter dwelling one was surprised to find a most attractive kitchen with gleaming cabinets, linoleum covered plank floor, and an attractive bedspread on the bed. Everything was as neat as a pin.

One day Hial and Mamie showed up at our place early in the morning. Frank and Hial went hunting and were lucky enough to find a nice fat buck not too far away. In no time he met his fate and was forthwith dressed out and brought into the house to be cut up and placed in canvas meat bags for storage in our cool cellar. About that time we spied a man from the American Ranch coming up the road on horseback. We knew he would have no compunctions about turning us in, so we must quickly disguise our activities.

Mamie emptied the contents of my laundry hamper and scattered dirty clothes over the carcass. The new visitor was met outside where the men sat on the sawhorse in the shade of the house to talk over whatever it is that men talk over. Meanwhile Mamie and I finished the meat project.

This was during the depression and wild meat was our main source of protein. Game wardens were very understanding and overlooked an occasional infringement of the law when they found one, but, on the other hand, they felt obligated to take action if someone was reported to them. You might ask, "Why not butcher one of your beeves?" Well, we wouldn't dare do that as the bankers kept close watch on their collateral.

Our early years at the ranch were anything but affluent. In my ignorance as a novice ranch woman, I guess I thought this was what all ranchers endured when they were starting out. In that respect, I had an advantage over my husband. After all, he was 30 years old when we were married, and in his youth had seen his father grow quite wealthy in the cattle business. I am sure it must have been difficult to live in the same area, do the same work as his family had done, but see practically no tangible returns.

In spite of financial limitations and lots of hard work, being a rancher in those days had its own compensations. I remember some of the things we enjoyed at the school section house. During the warm summer evenings we might see a glorious sunset reflected off the water as we took a dip in the river that had been warmed by the sun.

No one in the city, where cultured flower beds and manicured lawns are the norm, could have gotten more of a thrill than we did when our only healthy lilac bush bloomed profusely in the spring. It had been set out at a strategic place near the back porch, where it caught the drip from our monstrous solid oak ice box which sat just inside. The chunk of ice slowly melted and dripped down and out to water the lilac.

It was always a sad day when the last of the ice was gone from our icehouse, a well-insulated dugout which was packed with chunks of ice sawed from a pond in midwinter. This stored ice replenished the ice box and provided ice for the ice cream freezer on such special occasions as birthdays, the Fourth of July, or rare company from town.

Our homestead was on the south side of Powder River, which was not exactly convenient as the only road was on the north side. When the river was low we could ford it to get to the other side and the main road.

An alternative method, and the only way during the spring high water, was by way of a cable that Frank rigged up. The cable stretched across the river from one huge tree to another. From the cable we suspended a simple board seat on a pulley that rolled along the cable, transporting us from one side to the other, all the time swinging wildly. We zipped along at tremendous speed when going from the high bank below the house, but coming back home we laboriously pulled the seat along with a hand over hand method. Heavy gloves were a must.

We lived at the homestead for several years, during which time we had our family. Our first child, James Francis, was born May 19, 1933 in Buffalo. I had gone to Buffalo ahead of time as Frank was gone much of the time rounding up wild horses with neighboring ranchers, and did not want to leave me alone at the isolated homestead.

These horses, being some generations removed from their domesticated forebears, were a real challenge, not only to catch, but to train into an animal that was of any value as a cowboy's means of transportation.

In those days away from the ranch, I spent my time between my folks' place and Mother Davis's place. I felt wonderful and enjoyed immensely the long days of visiting with both of them. After nearly a month in Buffalo, I was at Mother Davis's and began to feel the contractions. She timed them right to the second, calling the doctor a few times before he decided to take action. Dr. Knebel came and took me to the hospital and a few hours later delivered my baby.

By that time Frank had arrived. He had been out with several other cowboys rounding up wild horses when he was informed that I was in the hospital. I think he broke the speed record coming into town, first on his trusty horse Socks and then in the Ford Truck, for it seemed that he was there in a very short time. Contrary to today's short stay, I was in the hospital for ten days. The total cost was $35, plus another $35 for the doctor.

The Community Hospital was owned by Nora Freeman. She had been a nurse for Dr. Knebel for a long time and decided to make her house into a hospital. As with many old houses, one must go through one room to get to another, and mine was in the dining room, between the living room and kitchen. At that time she did all of the cooking and also the laundry. I came to think a great deal of her, and my stay there was like being a guest someplace. She would often come and ask me what I would like for my meals. Her garden produced many fresh vegetables in season. There were no bells, not much privacy, no lab, and no delivery room.

There was no nursery in the hospital, however she kept a couple of cribs in the kitchen. She took care of all of the needs of the baby, bathing him and fixing the bottles. She'd dress him up in one of the many fancy little dresses made for him by relatives and friends. One morning she took him around to show him off to all of the other patients, and when she came back he was holding a carnation fast in his little hand, a gift from one of them.

After leaving the hospital I again spent many days with my mother and mother-in-law. It was almost a month before Frank came in to move his new family back to the ranch. I couldn't understand the delay until I got home and there on our back porch was a brand new kerosene-burning refrigerator. He had been waiting all that time to have it delivered from Montgomery Ward. It was the biggest luxury we had ever seen in our married lives. What a magnificent treat it was that summer to have ice to put in our lemonade, and how convenient to keep the baby's milk fresh. Whatever new thing we obtained was appreciated to the fullest because it was out of the ordinary.

Jim was a very good baby. His presence brought new meaning to our lives, as well as a little worry. We were both old enough to realize the tremendous responsibility we had in raising a child. There were many discussions as to methods of dealing with problems that we would surely encounter. We agreed that explanations are better than punishment in most cases. Another rule we adhered to was to back each other when discipline was necessary. We had a happy household with plenty of indulgence in the sharing of ideas and anything else that didn't cost money.

Two years later on April 17, 1935 our first daughter, Dorothy Ann, was born in the same little hospital. Frances Allison was born there on October 11, 1938, just a day shy of Frank's birthday. Frank had been certain that Allison would be born on his birthday, so she was a day old by the time he arrived in Buffalo from his gold prospect on the Big Horn Mountains.

That was our family. We were fortunate to have happy, healthy children. They all walked early and never crawled. Later I thought that was no doubt due to the condition of our plank floor. Who wants to get down on hands and knees on a splintery floor?

Dorothy and Jimmy in the Powder River

*   *   *

In the depression years trapping for furs was one means of securing a little extra cash. In the mid-30's

Frank was successful in trapping enough beaver to finance a vacation to Oregon and the Pacific Ocean.

I packed a steamer trunk which we placed between the front and back seats of our trusty little Model A sedan. With our bedding on top of the trunk and on the back seat, Jimmy and Dorothy had a perfect playpen.

There were few motels (we called them tourist cabins then) along the way, besides we felt they were beyond our means. Every night we set up a tent and cooked our dinner on a small wood-burning camp stove.

One evening, being especially tired, we decided to take a room at a hotel. Of course we never found one, and ended up making a forced camp in the dark of night. We could hardly sleep because of an indescribably bad odor, and discovered the next morning that we had camped next to a goat pasture!

At the Rogue River in Oregon some friendly people invited us to camp for a few days near their house. After the dry hills at Powder River we were enthralled by the lush environment along the Rogue River Valley. We saw many familiar plants, but in this moist climate they grew to a much greater size than we had ever seen. Blackberries grew profusely around our camp. Our friendly neighbor said, "Pick all you want, I never use them." Frank went to town and bought a dozen pint jars which I filled with blackberries and cooked on our little homemade stove, a tasty souvenir of our trip when we returned home. Frank also met a man who took him out fishing. They brought home a large salmon on which we dined royally.

Our "landlord" was also a woodworker who made beautiful bowls and vases from myrtlewood, which grew in a small area nearby. I still have one which is inscribed on the bottom: "A small area on the Pacific coast contains the world's supply of this rare and beautiful wood.

Centuries of slow maturing in the moist sea air have woven into its depths the romance of sea and sky, forest and mountain. The draftsman's art brings this gift of nature to you."

Our first view of the Pacific was thrilling. Frank had spent some time on the Atlantic coast, but the rest of us had never seen such a great expanse of water. My landlubber eyes kept searching for a spot of land somewhere on the far horizon.

* * *

During the summer of 1936 Mother Davis became quite ill. Her son Mark took her from Buffalo to his home in Casper where she was made as comfortable as possible in their beautiful house. She was well cared for with doctors and nurses on call. Her condition worsened, however, and one day we got a call to come to Casper. Our neighbors took Dorothy and Jimmy and we left for Casper in October of 1936. I think it must have been very hard for Frank to see his mother so utterly helpless, as she had always been a busy person.

We stayed a few days. Although Mother Davis was scarcely able to talk, I am sure she realized we were there. I tried to tell her something about the children, I hope she understood. That was the last time we saw her as she died not long after we returned to the ranch.

Frank was administrator of her estate which included land, some livestock, shares in a few investments, and a house full of very nice furniture. All of this had to be divided between the six children: three boys and three girls. Frank leaned over backwards to give everyone a fair share. Each was given a number and took his or her turn choosing an item from the household furnishings. After they were all sorted out, the rest of the possessions were liquidated. We breathed a sigh of relief when the last paper was signed and we were free to return to our own uncomplicated life.

The following spring Frank was eager for us to get back to his gold claims. These were located about 40 miles from the town of Ten Sleep, on the other side of the Big Horn Mountains from Buffalo. The last two miles took us over a tortuous sheepherder road. We then crossed a boggy creek and went up a precipitous, rocky incline which was just barely wide enough for the car. Even our abode, a tent house, looked pretty good to us after that journey.

The tent house walls were constructed of slabs of wood built up to about five feet above the plank floor. The roof was a canvas tent stretched across the top which we made on my Singer treadle sewing machine. Frank would pull the heavy material through as I guided it and treadled with my feet.

We stayed there through the summer and then moved back down to the homestead. The following summer was also spent in the tent house, and then in the fall Frank took me to Buffalo as I was soon expecting the birth of our third child. Soon afterwards the tent house burned down while Frank was working at the nearby gold prospect. Fall winds had blown the canvas door flap against the still hot stove and that was the end of our first mountain home.

After the birth of Allison we continued to live on the homestead and on the mountains until Jimmy started the first grade in 1939 at the Sussex country school. We then moved back to the school section house which was a small step closer to civilization and school.

I think Frank was reluctant to move away from the homestead, his very own ground where he could get on his trusty horse Socks and ride over the hills as free as the wind, as he checked the cow herd to see if any calves were separated from their mothers, whether there were any signs of coyotes, or whether the grass was becoming scarce and a move to another pasture might be required.

The school section house, winter 1939

At the same time, I was pretty well anchored at home with three small children and our primitive means of transportation across the river. So I was finding it hard to conceal my happy anticipation when I thought of moving back to "civilization."

We were fortunate that Frank was awarded the job of driving the school bus, which meant that Jim and later

Dorothy could board right at their door. This was an
advantage in cold weather, even if they did have to ride
the entire route before being deposited at the little
country school. For the school bus Frank bought a pickup,
built a wooden cover over the back, and put bench seats
along the sides.

It was a treat to live in a house with lots of room,
but it was a cold, cold place in the winter. The living room
was huge with a fireplace in one end which let in cold air
unless a roaring fire was going in it. At the other end was
a big pot-bellied stove in which we would pile wood and
coal until the sides were literally red hot. The immediate
surroundings of that stove were warm, but one could
stand close to it and freeze on one side while roasting on
the other.

The Wyoming winds had no trouble finding their
way between the logs. Water was again a problem.
Drinking and household water had to be hauled from a
water well at a neighboring ranch. The three years we
spent at that location saw some changes. We were feeling
more and more government pressures as that entity took
on a greater authority. There were programs designed to
better the living standards of citizens affected by several
years of depressed financial problems.

In the West cattle prices were low and the
Secretary of Agriculture evidently believed in the law of
supply and demand, even if the situation had to be
created artificially. That is just what he did. All ranchers
were ordered to slaughter a certain percent of their steers
but were not allowed to use the meat, for that would do
nothing for his economic law. This program would make a
short supply, but the demand would remain the same,
therefore, higher prices would ensue. Very good on paper
but no one had any money to buy higher priced beef, so
this episode went down as a black mark for the

Department of Agriculture. All we got out of it was less than $20 a head for the slaughtered animals.

With the help of his "brain trust," Roosevelt, through his New Deal, formulated and carried out some bold plans. He made some drastic changes in programs caring for the needy. He established the Public Works programs (PWA) and the Civilian Conservation Corps (CCC). He reorganized banks all over the country by declaring a moratorium on bank transactions for three days.

PWA paid some people to write historical articles for publication by the government. Out of work construction workers became part of the Works Progress Administration (WPA). CCC employees were put to work building Meadowlark Dam in the Big Horn Mountains. This period marked the beginning of government-financed projects which have continued to expand until people have come to depend more and more on government assistance.

By the mid 1930's people as a whole were beginning to feel a little more confident about the country when they saw that more jobs were available. The rancher and farmer were still hurting, however. Beef was still a luxury not in great demand and the country was experiencing a severe draught. Many ranchers and farmers were forced off their land.

As it became evident that the market for beef would remain poor and that restrictions would increase, we decided that we could do better in some other business. Frank put the ranch on the market, and we had it sold by the first of December and signed the papers on December 7, 1941, that fateful day in history that changed our lives and the World.

"No house should ever be <u>on</u> anything. It should be <u>of</u> the hill, belonging to it, so hill and house could live together each the happier for the other."   Frank Lloyd Wright

Chapter 10

An Aerie on the Big Horns

For years Frank had studied books on geology as related to the formations he had observed in his travels over the mountains. In 1935 he located an area about 40 miles south of Ten Sleep on the southern Big Horn Mountains which he thought looked promising for gold. We spent a few summers up there living in the tent house, which was quite satisfactory for our short summer stays.

In the summer of 1938 we decided it was time to build a cabin which would be more comfortable and permanent than our tent house.

Frank and my brother Lawrence cut and hauled logs from a pine forest up the mountain. The trees were cut and trimmed with a two-man timber saw and double bladed ax, loaded on the Model A truck, and hauled to the building site. Once there they were stripped of bark and each log cut to size and carefully notched near the end so that they fit together like children's Lincoln logs.

We gathered flat rocks which formed the foundation with a minimum of mortar. Before placing the logs Frank utilized his mining knowledge to blast and

The tent house

excavate a small pantry cellar at the middle of the cabin which would be accessed by a trap door in the floor. As the wall logs went up, the window and door openings were sawed in place.

Once the log walls had reached the roof line, large ridge logs were put in place using a system of ropes, pulleys, levers and ramps. The ridge log was extra long and of a larger diameter. Once it was in place and firmly secured with bridge spikes and braces, we celebrated with some time off and a toast with cold spring water and cookies. The large log would make a picturesque beam along the length of the ceiling. The floor and roof were made from lumber hauled in from a sawmill some distance over the top of the mountain.

Initially, we covered the roof with tar paper and several inches of soil to provide insulation, hoping that grass and plants would take root and anchor the dirt from the erosion of the wind. The soil proved too sandy, and no match for the winds, which sometimes lived up to their Wyoming heritage. Mortar chinking between the logs kept the wind out of the cabin and we were quite cozy with a thick bed of glowing embers in the iron stove.

The views from the cabin's three windows were spectacular - to the west one could watch a storm build over the distant Absaroka Mountains and work across the broad Big Horn Basin and up our mountain. Many times we would be above the clouds. Below them would probably be a storm, but at our elevation we had bright sun, giving us the appearance of being alone in our boundless world. To the south could be seen the distant sheep camps and bands of sheep scattered over the mountain valleys. To the east the mountain rose high above us, dominated by the Big Rock.

From these windows we saw elk, deer, mink and ermine. On a warm day rockchucks would be out sunning themselves on the granite outcrop near the cabin. Little striped chipmunks provided hours of entertainment with their antics. Sometimes we assisted in their shows by hanging an ear of corn on a string, which seemed to provide true entertainment for them as they leaped and gyrated to pull off the kernels of corn.

Wherever we went there were interesting places. We traveled miles exploring the little springs, groves of stately spruce trees and huge rock formations, including an enormous granite monolith the size of a six story building. This rock, which we called simply the Big Rock, was high on the mountains east of us and appeared to have been used as an Indian fortification of sorts. Rocks had been piled up around the top thereby providing

The Big Rock

an ideal defense and observation post. We had discovered a place where the rock could be scaled. The climb was worth the effort. Not only for the view, but we were rewarded by finding many arrowheads, agate chips and part of a clay pipe.

Our water supply was a most valuable asset. A spring 100 yards up from the cabin was dug out and a small platform built on which to stand while scooping up a bucket of clear, cold water. The water seemed to be the best tasting water we had ever experienced, especially after the hard water of the Powder River ranch.

A few feet below the spring was a box set down far enough so that the water ran through it, keeping our perishable food in excellent condition. A short distance below this was a stream where fishing was a thrill. I could take my pole down below the cabin, sit in the sun on a nice rock, throw in my line and catch enough fish in an hour or so for a meal.

My dad spent one summer with us. In the middle of July he hiked up the mountain east of the cabin and found a well-preserved snowdrift hidden next to a rocky ledge in a spruce grove from which he brought back enough snow to make ice cream with our hand-cranked freezer for my birthday. We left the freezer there that winter and in the spring found it practically gnawed to pieces by porcupines craving the salt.

We all enjoyed having Dad with us, especially the children, for he was a gentle, patient grandfather. We had the luxury of a milk cow that summer and Dad took on the job of cowherd and milker, no small duty. One day the cow (named Bossy' in line with her independent nature) left in search of a "bull friend" and Dad had to walk miles to fetch her back.

Dad always had some project to help improve our little home in the mountains. Jimmy (age 10) was enlisted by his granddad to build an outhouse from aspen logs, but the building was halted for awhile when Jim chopped his foot instead of a tree. We cleaned the wound with Lysol, taped it shut, and Dad made a crutch for Jim to limp around on for the next two weeks.

The summers we had on our mountain gave us a feeling of euphoria - our every mood was satisfied. As I stood by the west window mixing bread or washing dishes, my imagination soared as I gazed across the miles and miles of hills and valleys of the Big Horn Basin far below. There was such an utter feeling of space and freedom. If I were in an introspective mood, I would go out behind the cabin and sit on a favorite rock, so shaped that it made an unbelievably comfortable seat. Here I

Frank ready for prospecting

could sit and watch the chipmunks scurrying around in search of pine nuts, or watch the blue jay scolding me for invading his solitude, or there were the clouds, fascinating as they constantly changed.

Late in the fall of 1938, after we had disposed of our cattle on the homestead and leased our pasture to Meikes, we made preparations to spend the winter at our new little cabin in the Big Horns. Allison was two months old, Dorothy three years and Jimmy five. Jimmy would be entering school the next fall, so this was our last obligation-free year. We loaded the car to the gills and then some, as Frank had built a luggage holder at the back of the car (no storage trunks in those days). There we tied on my sewing machine which had been placed in a homemade crate.

We went by way of Casper. That meant a visit to the Mark Davis house where Winnie added to our already bulging load with a passel of Christmas gifts. We left there December 11 and drove the Nowood road over Cottonwood Pass on the mountains to the Holland Ranch. By the time we reached there it had started to snow quite heavily. We spent the night with this hospitable family.

By morning we abandoned the idea of taking the car any further, so loaded everything onto a heavy flat sled or drag used to haul heavy stuff around the farm. The men hitched up a big workhorse to the sled. Mrs. Holland came carrying rocks she had heated in the oven and wrapped in newspapers to keep our feet warm. We bundled Allison up in a sheepskin coat and were on our way.

We traveled on sled for six miles up the mountain, across snow deep enough to muffle every sound. I can't remember ever experiencing such utter quiet or such solitude. When we reached our destination we remained on the sled under our cozy wraps until Frank had a roaring fire going in the stove. We severed our last link with civilization when we gave the horse a slap on the rump and sent him down the mountain. I don't suppose he stopped until he reached his barn and bucket of oats.

Thus began the most unique four months of our lives. The snow continued to fall more heavily than usual so that travel by skis or snowshoes was our only method of transportation. This was no little task considering all of the canned milk Frank carried on his back from the Holland ranch to keep Allison well-fed, in addition to the groceries we needed. At Christmas time everyone who knew our circumstances had the best of intentions when they sent many extra packages, but I am sure Frank was not overcome with happiness when he spied all the extra freight.

Our little dwelling had a good linoleum-covered floor and windows on every side except the north. The northwest window presented an unobstructed view all the way to the Pryor Mountains in Montana. This distant horizon provided all the requisites for the most beautiful sunsets ever seen. Not a telephone pole, not a smoke stack, not a single sign of man, just the faraway hills whose outlines were softened by a constant Bierstadtian haze, were between us and the glowing colors of the sky.

Besides the gorgeous sunsets, the cloud formations were spectacular, especially when a storm was brewing. Occasionally from our sunny perch we could watch such a storm develop and sweep across the lowlands, resembling a giant brush being wielded by an invisible hand.

At other times we had a feeling of being all alone on an island on top of the world when all the hills and valleys below us were completely hidden from view by a solid cloud cover. Years later we were to experience somewhat the same sensation when viewing cloud cover from a jet window at 20,000 feet elevation.

In spite of our close quarters our cabin was adequate. The kitchen corner contained a cabinet with an enameled metal countertop above the flour and sugar bins, a wall-mounted, heavy wood crate whose lid hinged down to form a work counter covered with oilcloth. Above the cabinet orange crate cupboards with curtains held the dishes. Completing this area was a cast iron cookstove which was also the only source of our heat. The window next to the work counter looked west over the vast Big Horn Basin and I never tired of the scene while cooking.

Next to the "kitchen" a homemade rough lumber table covered with gaily colored oilcloth, two folding chairs and a bench made up the dining area which looked out upon the wonderful pastoral scene to the south. Our only "easy" chair was an automobile bucket seat resurrected from a wrecking yard. A sewing machine, washstand and two double-wide bunk beds completed the furnishings in our one room 12 by 20 foot abode.

Sawing wood for winter

The sewing machine crate, with a little working over, made quite a snug baby crib. We had no mechanical plumbing problems except to keep the water bucket full, the slop bucket empty, and a path shoveled to the little outhouse. Our washer consisted of a tub and washboard. The dryer was an outside clothesline, which was all too often impractical, being blocked by a large snowdrift which required me to climb up the drift and reach down to hang up the laundry. The inside line seemed to be always full of drying mittens and leggings. All this contributed to our high humidity, which became quite evident on a very cold day. When the outside door was opened, the sudden blast of cold air would create a distinctly visible cloud which rolled across the floor and evaporated upon contact with the stove.

The small spring was a remarkable source of all our household water. It had been dug out and deepened until the pool was probably five feet in diameter and a couple of feet deep. No matter what the weather, the water remained at a constant 40 degrees and all who tasted it declared it the best water ever.

By gradually building up snow blocks around the edges and dousing them with water on cold days, we soon had a beautiful ice wall. An opening was left on one side with steps cut into the icy slope to the water. By using a little igloo-type architecture we eventually had a covered spring, the walls a gorgeous gem-like blue when viewed from the inside towards the light. The icy formations formed by the constant condensation of the steam on the walls and ceiling presented a phenomenon certainly comparable to, if not surpassing, those commercial ice caves one must share with hordes of paying tourists. Carrying water became a pleasurable anticipation instead of a chore.

One of the biggest problems we faced was to keep ourselves supplied with the necessary requirements of proteins and vitamins. Fortunately, our fifty pound tin container was practically full of flour and we had a good supply of cereals, but meat was hard to get. On account of the greater than average snowfall, the game animals had moved down to better forage. We scarcely saw so much as a rabbit.

Every week or two Frank found it necessary to don handmade snowshoes or long wood skis and take off down the mountain on that laborious trip to the ranch six miles away. He would then drive the Model A eight miles further to the small country store to replenish the baby's supply of canned milk and to get our mail and whatever else we needed. On a few occasions he dragged a homemade toboggan behind him and tugged it back up again packed with supplies. I'm sure there must have been moments on such a trip when he had second thoughts as to the wisdom of the recent family move.

The trip down required very little effort. We would watch from the cabin window and in no time at all he would be a tiny speck against the white expanse of snow, and finally out of sight behind a distant knoll. I always had the utmost confidence in Frank's ability to make the trek safely; it never entered my mind to worry and I am sure that he felt just as confident or we wouldn't have been on the mountain that winter.

The return trip was not so fast or easy. The 30 to 40 pound load he was carrying, and the steady uphill climb was not only strenuous but required a certain amount of dexterity to manipulate those skis uphill. He finally devised a sort of brake by fastening a sawed off barn hinge on the back end of the ski in such a way that when the ski slipped back, the hinge would drop down and dig into the snow, then straighten out again when the ski went forward.

The little Nowood store didn't sell meat or produce. On rare occasions we were able to get a little meat from the Holland Ranch, however not often enough to include it in our daily diet. We did get meat-hungry, and on one afternoon Frank shot a porcupine and butchered it. We hung it on the north side of the cabin on a ridge log to age. The meat was light-colored, resembling a young pig.

When we finally decided it was ready to cook, we quartered it, placed it in a roaster, and put it in the oven. We expected an aroma reminiscent of fresh pork to soon come wafting from the oven. It didn't. When we took it from the stove and sliced a piece off it still looked so much like pork we expected it to taste like it. It didn't. In fact, it didn't taste much like anything and was tough besides. By grinding the meat and adding all the seasonings we could find, we made a meal from it. Needless to say, I never did add this to my list of favorite recipes.

We did have some canned meat and tried to keep beans and cheese on hand. We never seemed to be able to make our eggs last from one trip to another. Even so, with our limited diet we never felt underfed or undernourished, and in spite of it no one had so much as a cold all winter, and the baby Allison was the happiest and healthiest child one could wish for.

Christmas was special that year. Most of the tree decorations and many of the presents we supplied ourselves with unsuspected resourcefulness. The trips down the slope just before the holidays brought almost too many packages - all from well-meaning friends and relatives who no doubt were feeling sorry for the isolated family in the mountains.

By the time the tree was set up and trimmed with strings of popcorn and chains made from colored pages cut from magazines, and the rag doll, game board and other homemade goodies were ready to be brought from their hiding places, everyone was in a holiday mood. As a matter of fact, we seemed to have a deeper feeling of the true Christmas spirit with the absence of any commercial flimflam.

With the lovely clothes, candy, toys, and other gifts, all of which had been brought up that mountain with such great effort, and with the products of our own hands, the children thought it the most marvelous Christmas ever. So it was, for what did they have to compare it with? Certainly no fancy store windows or envied demonstrations of the more affluent neighbors down home. Early Christmas morning Frank skied close by the cabin with his skis spread far apart; when the children spotted the "sleigh" tracks it was proof-positive that Santa had found us!

One of Jim's gifts was a pair of skis. We had a little knoll that today would be called a Mickey Mouse slope where he and I would don our skis and practice. One day on the way to the slope he dropped one of his skis and away it went down the mountainside, weaving in and out among the trees like a live thing. We watched it disappear, with a mixture of awe at its speed and dexterity, and with despair as we thought it gone for good. However we had the spot pretty much in mind where we saw it last, and after floundering down through the snow for a couple of hundred yards, there it was, having miraculously reached the "angle of repose" rather than slithering on down the two miles to Lost Creek. On our way down to get the ski we were rewarded by catching a brief glimpse of a weasel, resplendent in his beautiful snow-white, black-tipped ermine coat.

As the days grew longer and warmer, the snow disappeared from the south sides of the buildings and the older children spent more time outdoors. They were out for countless hours making doll houses by laying rocks on the ground to form rooms, and roads and bridges for make-believe trucks. These vehicles were nothing more than blocks of wood with a very faint resemblance to car bodies. Their dolls required a stretch of the imagination also, as most of them were sticks of wood with a face drawn on one end.

Some of these toys had more of an appeal to them than their factory made articles. Their boughten ones having been made in a mold were just what they were, while the crude homemade toys required an imagination to supply the details. The latter could be as elaborate as they wished, and certainly their mental inventions were entirely uninhibited.

Imagine, if you will, a couple of brothers, probably not even carved from the same branch, but who were very real. Their names (also invented by the children) were Corsikine and Mercimine. These characters and their activities were discussed and worried over by Jim and Dorothy as if they had been real people.

One day we received a letter from my brother Bear saying he would be glad to accept our invitation to spend a few weeks on the mountains with us. The masonry work at which he had been employed was at a standstill due to cold weather.

It was shortly after Christmas when he was met by Frank at the Holland ranch, handed a pair of snowshoes, and forthwith initiated into the first of many strenuous exercises he was to experience during his stay with us. The men planned to cut fence posts and sell them in the spring, thereby bringing in a little cash. Of course a goodly share of each workday was spent locating and sawing enough wood for our stove, as we had to keep a fire going most of the time. We also had a small shop which was put into regular use as a bedroom with the arrival of Bear, and its 30-gallon oil drum stove also devoured lots of wood.

In the matter of the fence posts, the first step was to locate a dead tree which was still good and solid. This was sawed off as far down towards the ground as possible, the branches trimmed close to the trunk, and then dragged down the slope to the cabin. There, it was sawed and split into desired sizes. The following summer I found some of the stumps standing close to four feet high, giving evidence of the depth of the snow the previous winter.

For the most part, the snow supplied a hard surface for walking. Very rarely did we break through the top crust, except in the wooded areas where the footing wasn't too reliable. More than once we were caught unawares and suddenly found ourselves in a very awkward position with one leg up to the hip in snow and the rest of the body sprawled on top of the drift. Believe me, it was no small feat to extricate the buried member from such a disadvantageous position.

We had a variety of weather, with many beautiful days. On one such day Bear announced at the breakfast table that he would like to take a hike east over the ridge towards the headwaters of Powder River to see if, perchance, he might come upon something that would add to our larder. I'm sure he felt such a jaunt would be a welcome change from the day-to-day regimen. He didn't wish to be burdened with anything to carry, and as he planned to be back before dark, he took just a couple of pancakes left from breakfast for his lunch.

After receiving directions from Frank as to how to locate an old line camp cabin in case he found it necessary to spend the night, he took off amid cheery farewells from the children and admonitions from us to be careful and "bring home the bacon."

The children were playing outside making little tunnels in the snow. Frank was at the shop grinding rock to make a test, I was mending the arm on a rag doll while I watched the baby playing happily on the floor in a patch of sunshine. Such a quiet, peaceful atmosphere had us feeling a bit drowsy when we were suddenly aroused from our lethargy by the children who rushed into the house with "br-r-r-s" and "O-O-O-Oh's," saying they were freezing. I teased them about it until I checked the thermometer. To my amazement it had plunged twenty degrees in a very short while.

I became concerned about my brother, especially when I went out to the shop to seek reassurance from my husband. The minute I stepped outside I could feel that sharp north wind and noticed an ominous bank of clouds building up fast in the north. We tried to convince ourselves that, no doubt, Bear had found his shelter before the wind came up. All we could do was hope our conjectures were correct and turn our energies to keeping ourselves comfortable. By 5:30 that evening the temperature had dropped 60 degrees, from plus 40 to minus 20.

We sat through the evening, each of us trying to appear absorbed in our reading while actually I found myself going over and over a simple paragraph and still not knowing what it was about. We finally gave up and went to bed, as we felt the smart thing would be for us to get a good rest and be ready for the next day and whatever it might bring.

Needless to say, we had a hard time getting to sleep. Many unanswerable questions presented themselves. As I listened to the wind howling like a banshee and snow coming down harder and harder, all together adding to the perils of the wayfarer, I wondered, "What if he were really lost?" We would never be able to see his tracks after this terrific wind and new snow. "What if he didn't find that cabin?" He would never survive outside on a night like this.   Although we had no wind chill factor charts we were fully aware of the inability of the human body to withstand for long a strong wind accompanied by sub-zero temperatures.

At long last sleep overtook us, and when we awoke the next morning the sun was bright, the sky was a beautiful blue and there was not a whisper of a breeze.

Everything was so very peaceful and quiet it seemed as if all Nature had fallen and was lying limp in a state of utter exhaustion after such a fiendish night. We all kept turning our eyes to that bit of the horizon on the ridge east of us searching for a welcome figure. Eleven o'clock came, still no sign. My husband had just about decided to take a thermos of coffee and start out for the shelter cabin when Jim shouted, "There he is! There he is!" and sure enough the traveler was returning. As he came closer we could hardly recognize him, and there was no doubt he had had a fire going somewhere. The evidence was all over him. His face, hands, and clothes were as black as coal. He was exhausted, starved, and well-smoked, but otherwise seemingly none the worse for his excursion. He had two fine looking grouse slung over his shoulder.

Apparently, as the wind came up, blowing snow caused him to get off on the wrong trail. He thereby missed the good cabin, but found part of a shack which contained a broken-down stove but no chimney. Building a fire on the open grates of a stove, even though it was minus a top and a flue, was a far cry better than keeping a fire going on the ground someplace. He kept from freezing by burning every piece of wood he could break up, including the remains of the furniture and part of the walls of the dilapidated cabin.

He had had a change of scenery, all right, and I'm sure when he came over the hills and saw our sturdy cabin with smoke spiraling from the chimney, he was very glad to be back. He was ready for food, soap and water, and rest, which we made available in that order.

I then proceeded to dress the grouse. Of course they contained no globs of fat and all they had in their craws were pine needles. We boiled them with a bit of vinegar in the water. After they were tender, we took the meat off the bones and made a curry sauce in which we simmered the pieces of fowl. This we served over rice. We all concluded that the finest gourmet cook in the country couldn't have turned out a more tasty dish.

I have been forced to conclude since then that some people nowadays seldom enjoy the complete satisfaction of having their wants supplied, whether it be food, entertainment, or material acquisitions, simply because all of these things are so readily available before we hardly know we want them. We become satiated to the point of becoming blasé about everything.

Our ingenuity was taxed in other fields, also, as we were called upon to provide something new in the line of games, dolls and other toys with which to keep the youngsters entertained. Empty spools were at a premium, as well as every bit of cardboard that could be salvaged from packages or grocery boxes. There was many an argument over who was going to get the next empty cereal box. By taking seven empty milk cans, covering them with old socks so they could be sewed together, and covering the assembled cans with material from the rag bag, we had a neat little stool.

The lack of perfection in these homemade articles was more than compensated for by the fertile imagination of the recipients. In one of the boxes brought from the old ranch on an earlier occasion were some *St. Nicholas* magazines dating from 1906. Their stories and illustrations were charming and provided literary fare few children were privileged to have.

For Valentine's day we used a variety of material including colored covers from magazines, foil from tea boxes, paints made from cake coloring, and used envelopes. Everyone got into the act with the results being quite diverse, to say the least.

We kept in touch with the world somewhat by listening to our radio. A six-volt battery supplied the power. Frank devised our own wind generator to keep the battery charged, as we had no motor driven vehicle to do the job. Wind, on the other hand, was a more than plentiful commodity.

Wind powered generator

Easter was approaching, and since we had been unable to get any extra eggs the last few trips down the mountain, we were becoming a bit concerned as to where the Easter bunny was going to get eggs. As it turned out, someone else was a little bit concerned also. A few days before Easter, Frank came back from one of his regular trips for supplies with a couple of extra packages from way across the mountains. My mother had made an angel food cake and mailed it to us along with a large box of oatmeal. Oatmeal?? Yes, and very strategically packed in it so that none of them touched each other were a dozen beautiful big white eggs in perfect condition.

As I wrote my mother later to tell her how much we appreciated her thoughtfulness in sending such wonderful Easter gifts, it occurred to me that those eggs and that cake had made an incredible journey to reach us. To begin with, mother no doubt packed them with great care one evening. Presumably, my father took them the three miles to Buffalo the next morning when he went to work. After being mailed there, they went on by rural delivery to Sheridan where they were put on the Burlington train and sent to Billings, at least 160 miles away.

They were then transferred to the southbound train and made the journey to Manderson, another 150 miles or so, where the rural mail carrier picked them up and took them to Bonanza, 12 miles east. Again they were transferred, this time to the Ten Sleep rural mail truck and taken to Ten Sleep, adding another thirty-some miles. Here, the mail was sorted again and sent R.F.D. to the Nowood Post office 40 miles on, with still 12 miles to go by whatever means of transportation could be supplied by the Hollands and us. Most of this journey was made in unheated vehicles, but the products were in perfect condition when they arrived.

As the weeks went by we were becoming more self-sufficient and I found, upon analyzing my feelings about rejoining civilization, that I was a bit reluctant to give up our utter freedom. Nevertheless it was time we resumed our normal life along with its problems, pleasures and interesting associations we were bound to have as we reintroduced ourselves to neighbors and schools. The latter would become a vital part of our life very soon.

Our time spent up there, so isolated from people, will long be remembered. Probably the most outstanding difference between this and a more gregarious existence was the utter lack of outside influence. As a result, we all learned to place our own true values on things.

Such a unique experience would be impossible now, 60 years later. Snowmobiles, TV, short wave radios, and other modern inventions would bring this world to our door whether we wished it or not.

Chapter 11

After the Ranch

The move from the ranch in 1941, I am sure, must have been a rather traumatic move for Frank, as the old Davis ranch was bound to contain many memories to one who had lived his entire life on or close to the premises. As for my sentiments, I really could see no reason for staying there. I felt that any move would be to our advantage. There was nothing in this community for anyone who wasn't in the cattle business or a farmer. Now we were neither.

We opted for Casper for our first move, as there should be work there. My mother came down and stayed for a couple of days with the children while Frank and I looked for a house. We were fortunate in finding one on South Jackson, not far from school. We forthwith packed the truck and moved. We parked the piano at Kaycee and didn't retrieve it for two years.

We welcomed the advantages in Casper, such as hot and cold running water, a bathroom with a big tub, an automatic stove, and people who lived nearby. The latter, although not the really neighborly types we had enjoyed on the ranch, were nevertheless someone to talk to. Frank got a job with a fur company buying furs from trappers, who were plentiful during the depression. It was a living but not a lavish one. Before long he entered the ranks of war related employees, working on the construction of buildings.

Frank's brother Mark lived in Casper. He and his wife were wonderful to us while we lived there. "Aunt Winnie" was high on the list of the children's relatives as visits to their magnificent plantation style home on Center Street were most welcome diversions. Our city life was short-lived, though, as we moved to Thermopolis in 1942.

During this time Frank was still involved in construction work. I gave some music lessons in Thermopolis as well as serving as organist at the Episcopal church. These occupations provided ways of meeting some interesting people who were greatly appreciated by one who had so recently come from a life of more or less seclusion.

When school summer vacation started we took off for our mountain home again. We liked that simple and uncluttered life very much, and spent the summer on the mountains at our comfortable cabin. The children were old enough to get a great delight from exploring faraway places, out of earshot from the home base.

They became expert climbers and enduring hikers, which has been a source of enjoyment for all of them ever since. They had many more play areas than on the rough sagebrush covered hills of the ranch. A grove of enormous spruce trees provided little secret rooms under their branches. The soil was sandy and clean, admirable for building roads or Jimmy's forts. The various sizes and shapes of the many rocks stimulated their imaginations and they became houses, chairs, cars or whatever was needed. Corsikine and Mercimine lived on!

Dorothy had a certain rock she called the Queen's chair. She took me over to try it out one day - I couldn't believe how comfortable it was. It looked out over the miles of mountain valleys to the south.

Dorothy, Allison and Jimmy on the Rocks

When I attended school in Chicago in 1924-25, my roommate was Willah Burrows from Boca Raton, Florida; she had always been fascinated by the West. In the summer of '43 I had a letter from her from Laramie where she had attended summer school. She had a yen to see the West from a different viewpoint than the campus at the University provided. Since we had corresponded often she knew we were on the mountains, so wrote that she was making plans to come up to our part of the country before returning to Florida.

I was more than a little concerned as I could hardly picture my citified artist friend enduring the rugged, primitive life we were experiencing. I wrote and painted as accurate a picture as I could of what she could expect. That seemed to encourage rather than discourage her. She wrote that she had looked at the map carefully and found that by taking the bus to Worland she could hop on the mail truck and go to Ten Sleep, then on with the mail carrier to the Nowood store where we went to get our mail.

There seemed to be no deterring her, so we made preparations for her arrival. Frank drove to the Nowood store to meet her with a bit of uneasiness. However, by the time they got to the cabin they were good friends. She had quite a story to tell us of her trip. When she got to Worland she discovered to her dismay that the Ten Sleep mail truck did not go to Worland, but picked up the mail for Ten Sleep at Manderson, a village 30 miles north. Willah had been deposited at the Washakie Hotel, and with their kind assistance she got a ride with a trucker who was taking a load of coal to the Ten Sleep school. By the time they reached town she knew all about his family, and since he was a native, a lot of interesting history of the area.

Ten Sleep

In the small town of Ten Sleep it wasn't hard for her to make connections with the mail carrier, who also happened to be an interesting conversationalist.

Willah made herself at home and took to our very different and far-from-affluent lifestyle as if she had always lived so. She couldn't wait to try her luck at making a cake on our old fashioned wood cookstove. She was so proud of the finished product. Frank told her they would likely see deer if she wanted to get up before 5 o'clock. She was right there with her camera.

One day we drove to Deep Creek and hiked down a steep canyon to go fishing at our favorite fishing hole below an idyllic waterfall. The descent into the canyon was strenuous, and of course the climb out even more so. We certainly were never aware that we had a "green horn" along. We thoroughly enjoyed her stay and all of us hated to see her go back down the mountain.

The Falls on Deep Creek

Ten Sleep, a village with a population of 320 and about 40 miles from the cabin, was the closest town, so we decided to look for a house there. We liked the town and found a comfortable house to rent for the school year. Our move down to civilization that fall proved to be our last major move as a family entity. We rented the house for two years and in the meantime bought a lot and built a small house which was home for almost fifty years.

Although we practiced frugality from necessity while the children were growing up, they maintain to this day that they never felt poor. I found that many of the refinements of life needn't be denied for lack of money.

Sunday Dinner

Every Sunday, birthday and holiday meant covering the oilcloth dining table with a linen table cloth, setting on the best dishes and silver. Everyone was expected to practice good manners. Each of these occasions would be special. Perhaps events such as these helped create a false illusion of prosperity that lingered longer in memory than any material denials might have.

When the children were in school we loved our mealtime discussions. Their father would often bring up a question about anything from geography, to fractions, to the Civil War. If they couldn't answer, out came the encyclopedia, circa 1922, an investment I had made while teaching. It could provide answers to most questions providing it wasn't something that happened after World War I.

Jim and his dad loved to talk rocks, which I am sure gave our son his lasting interest in geology which has served him well. Dorothy was partial to trivia (the game hadn't been invented), and it was hard to get the best of her on a geography quiz. When she was in the 5th or 6th grade she could name all the states and most of their capitals. Allison was hard to stop in mathematics. She has put that to good use in her occupations in the business world.

*Allison, Jim, Frank, Verna and Dorothy - **1966***

Chapter 12

The Fencing Camps

Cattle ranching became more complex as the open range disappeared and government leases became a major factor in much of the west. In Wyoming 50% of the land is public (federal) lands. Ranches are seldom large blocks of contiguous land, but irregular checkerboards of various private owners and federal and state lands.

To keep the cattle of various owners on the appropriate land, to separate summer range from winter forage, and to protect areas from overgrazing required hundreds of miles of range fence to be built. These fences usually followed surveyed plat lines and as such cut across ravines, forests, canyons and rivers. They were constructed of wood and steel posts with barbed or woven wire.

It was quite an art to firmly set the posts in often rocky ground and get the wire taut. In the cold of winter, wires on a properly built fence would almost strum like a banjo. They controlled the cows, but deer and elk had no problem in leaping over them; only us humans out for a cross country walk or hunting cursed them. We were forced to carefully climb over using the 5 or so strands of barbed wire as steps, or, if the bottom wire was high enough, one could slither underneath being careful not to slide over a cactus patch. Either way there were risks involved!

Ten Sleep is primarily a ranching community, so there was a lot of fence to build and replace. Frank found a steady source of work in contracting fence building and soon built a reputation of building fence that was top quality. Because the jobs were often in remote parts of the mountains or the lower badlands, he often set up a camp near the job site; this saved him two or three hours a day of travel time.

He built a small sheepherder style covered wagon which contained a double bed, a small cast iron cookstove and a pull-out dining table/desk. When not busy teaching and after the children were grown I would join him at camp. The variety of camps provided an unending parade of wildlife and their young, changing seasons with the greening of grass, the blooming of flowers, and all types of weather. It's too bad we didn't keep better notes and write a book on the joys of fencing! But it was hard work.

In the badlands, the dry, often barren, someplaces sagebrush draped hills that form a large part of the Big Horn Basin, a rain brought everything to a standstill. The clayey soil turned to sticky gumbo, building up on boots and tires and making any type of travel almost impossible. On those days we kept busy reading or baking bread for the busier work days.

Even though there are no trees in the badlands, there is a more built-in beauty; the rock formations are not only banded with reds and yellows and whites, but the wind had carved sandstone bluffs into a literal fantasy land of shapes, from giant toadstools to honeycombed caves. The term badlands referred to the lack of water more than anything else, sometimes ranchers had to haul water to their sheep and cattle.

There was a prairie dog town next to one of our badlands camps on Nowater Creek (a dry ravine as the name implies). These fat little animals quickly adjusted to our presence and resumed their normal lifestyle, which we soon found to be much more complex and varied than we could have imagined. We soon recognized individual personalities and laughed at a group of "gossips" that got together on one of the small hills next to a burrow. We gave names to the most notable characters. One we named Margaret after a Ten Sleep gossip (now deceased) who sagged in much the same places as the chubby little prairie dogs.

One summer we had a large contract with the Bureau of Land Management to build fence in the badlands southwest of Ten Sleep. The grazing lessor had a cattle tending camp, called a line cabin, in the area and invited us to use it while we were working there. That sounded great as our wagon was quite cramped and one had to sit while working at the stove.

The kitchen of the cabin had been used fairly recently and was not in bad shape, with a large wood-burning cookstove, shelves, table and even chairs. A door to the bedroom was closed, and when I ventured in there I found that there was already a tenant; on the bare bedsprings there was a huge pile of stuff . . . twigs, scraps of paper, empty rifle cartridges, some nails and on the very top of this eighteen inch high mountain of junk was an ironical touch - a mouse trap! Much like a cherry on top of a chocolate sundae! Next to the door a square two gallon oil can had been opened up on one side to hold kindling, and on top of the fine wood was a nicely arranged bed of green leaves. My deduction that this was a mother pack rat's accouchement proved to be correct in light of following developments.

I cleaned off and washed the bedsprings which, with three thicknesses of tarp placed on them, made a comfortable bed. That night I was aware of some feeble squeaking in the room. The next day I investigated further and discovered the mama pack rat and three babies back in the corner, on top of a high shelf with hooks on the bottom that served as the bedroom's wardrobe. I didn't disturb the family, as neither Frank nor I were touchy about having wild critters around as long as they stayed in their own territory. Evidently the mother didn't feel the same about us.

The next evening we were sitting in the kitchen reading by the yellow light of the lantern when we heard a small disturbance. We sat very quietly and presently here came mother rat past the open bedroom door headed for a hole that had been gnawed in the partition between the bedroom and the kitchen, ignoring the open door. She had a baby in her mouth, one was riding piggyback, and the third had a secure hold on mother's tail with its mouth. It was quite a show. The mother and her entrained brood made their way past the stove, up the logs, and across the room on a log to a high cupboard and on to the top of that where she deposited her family. Well, at least they were out of the bedroom.

Earlier that spring a cowboy's family had used the cabin for a time and the mother and daughter had apparently spent some time in attempting to make the kitchen a bit more livable by adding shelf paper to the rough wood cupboards and nailing cardboard from boxes to the wall logs and across the ceiling. This made up in cleanliness and as a wind barrier to what it perhaps lacked in generally accepted decor.

By the time we arrived the cardboard had sagged and lost what little decorative appeal it might have had. It was most unsightly. One day I took a hammer and began to rip the cardboard loose from the ceiling. To my amazement the whole ceiling came down, bringing with it the pack rat's entire food cache. She had stored, slice by slice, several loaves of bread in that made-to-order pantry.

When I recounted the story to the camp tender who stopped by a few days later, he said, "Well, that solves a mystery. I knew I had delivered bread to my herder, but it was late when I got here so I left the boxes of groceries in the pickup until morning. I didn't notice anything was missing until the herder chided me for not bringing any bread!" The herder had slept in his wagon and was unaware of the frenzied activity that night.

In the mountains we could often camp by a stream or in a green meadow where the wildlife was abundant, with the backdrop of a wonderful mountain view. Often we would look out of the wagon early in the morning and see elk or deer grazing just steps away. A dinner of trout could be had by dangling a hook in a small creek next to the camp.

We had just moved to a new location on the southern Big Horns and Frank was off to survey a fence location; I was in the wagon enjoying the delightful breeze and doing absolutely nothing but listening to the constant little mountain noises and half-dozing, when I glanced out the little window over the bed and saw a figure moving at a fast pace up through the large meadow towards me. As he approached I could see he was a small man with a very determined demeanor to his stride. I wondered what in the world was the reason for this visit.

I had not long to wait before he arrived and looked in the door. I'll never know what was on the tip of his tongue, for he was so flabbergasted at seeing a woman in a sheepwagon that he was speechless for a moment, his determined anger diverted. He was a small man, with a thatch of grey hair above a clean cut face, his clothes a bit worn but very clean. He introduced himself as Frank Fisher, telling me that he lived in a cabin a couple miles distant.

He explained that he was watching the pasture for a rancher friend, and thought we might be trespassing with sheep. He had no car but depended on ranchers in the area to deliver his groceries. He seemed satisfied when I told him what we were doing and shortly headed back for his cabin. A little later I was surprised to see him approaching again. This time he was carrying a mess of fresh trout, eager to make amends for his initial abruptness, saying only that he did a lot of fishing.

We were always careful not to park our camp wagon under the tallest trees as lightning storms were often severe in the high country. Unfortunately, some of the rancher's horses didn't take the same precautions and after one terrific storm, which we watched in all its fury from the wagon, the rancher came by with the sad news that two horses, including his favorite saddle horse, had been killed by lightning.

The western slope of the Big Horns is incised with many spectacular canyons and rugged breaks. The scattered pines are in stark contrast to the white walls of the canyons, and there are always signs of old Indian encampments such as teepee rings, stone chippings and even arrowheads, stone knives and axes. The limestone formations also yielded lots of fossils of ocean dwelling plants and mollusks. Our camps in this area were never boring, even after a hard day of building fence there was a strong urge to explore the rugged terrain for its treasures.

One of these camps was located near the head of aptly named Canyon Creek near Big Trails (a post office in earlier days) where Frank and his crew were building several miles of stock drive fence. A stock drive is a fenced-in cattle and sheep trail for herds being moved to mountain pastures in the spring and down in the fall. Our teenage daughter Dorothy was spending some time with her girlfriend at the father's summer cow camp, a nice cabin over the top of the mountain and a few miles away from our fencing camp. Dorothy planned to join the rest of us at our camp by getting a ride with her girlfriend's family. They were going on to town, so she had them let her out near where she thought our camp was. After almost a day of hiking and with darkness approaching she still hadn't found us.

With nightfall it began to get cool so she emptied the contents of her suitcase on the ground under a tree and made a bed where she spent a long and mostly sleepless night. At dawn she could hear animals cropping the grass and with a little more light could see several deer very close by. As the sun rose she packed up her suitcase and started walking again. In a short time she came over a small hill right into our camp. Hurrying down to the wagon she found the door locked. We had gone to town for supplies. Disappointed and tired, but somewhat relieved, she rested for a while then walked down the road a couple of miles to a cabin where the rancher fed her her first meal since the morning before. When we returned a day later we were more than a little surprised to find her there and even more amazed at her story.

Granddaughter Gail at badlands camp

Chapter 13

Back To Teaching

I was out in the yard of our rental house in Ten Sleep one sunny spring day in 1944 when a man came up and introduced himself as Superintendent of Schools. He went on to say that one of the teachers had left and he needed a substitute to finish the year. I told him I doubted that I would meet the qualifications, at which point he asked if I had ever taught. When I replied in the affirmative he said, "You're qualified." So I started the next Monday.

I finished the year as the 5th and 6th grade teacher, and then was rehired for another two terms. It was a little difficult to teach all three of my children, which I did during that period. They were good students, but I dared not give them special dispensations lest I be accused of showing favoritism.

During the third year of teaching Frank was home quite a bit, which greatly alleviated my responsibilities around the house. He saw that there was plenty of wood and coal for the heating stove and he was a very good laundry man. My neighbor said he hung out the whitest laundry on the block! It wasn't long after that that he started fencing work on many ranches in the area. That business was most successful, and he kept at it for several years.

After I quit teaching regularly, I substituted for many years and worked steadily with the music department. It expanded tremendously while our kids were in school - there had been nothing when we started. I taught music to both upper and lower grades and received such a tremendous response that it was a very gratifying job.

During the time I was teaching middle grades a band teacher from a neighboring town came in and held meetings with students, parents and teachers about starting a band in Ten Sleep. He brought in charts illustrating various instruments - some of the students hadn't known the difference between a trombone, a clarinet, or a trumpet. Now they saw the possibility of really holding an instrument and learning to play it.

I have never seen such an overwhelming response to a new concept. In no time at all, 35 to 40 students from grade school and high school were outfitted with instruments and attending band practice. Within two years we were being recognized at local festivals. Up until that time the only students who got to go on trips and visit other schools were the athletes. The band trips opened up many new experiences for these Ten Sleep students.

During these years I also taught piano at home. We had occasional recitals that would draw a sizable crowd of Ten Sleepers. Social functions were few and far between, and our town was seldom a stopover for professional entertainment.

All things considered, I look back at the years in Ten Sleep as fruitful. I think we all gained something from our experiences there. Jim graduated from high school with a scholarship to the University of Wyoming, presented by the county commissioners; Dorothy fell in love her senior year and married Dick Redland, a rancher and native of Ten Sleep, and Allison graduated with honors and also received a scholarship to the University.

All of the children demonstrated creativity that developed out of necessity when they were small. Jim has written many fascinating travelogues of his journeys to many parts of the world. Allison is using her appreciation of design and color in her home interior business. Dorothy has become quite well-known in the southwest for her watercolor and oil paintings.

Our family saw many changes in the next few years - Dorothy and Dick had a daughter, Deanna, so we were now grandparents. Allison went to the University for two years and then took a teaching position at a rural school 35 miles west of Thermopolis, where she met and married Keith Davis. Jim worked summers for geological firms and received his degree in geology in 1957. In the meantime, he married Dorothy Ann Maret of Thermopolis, a student at the University majoring in business.

In 1959 while Allison was teaching at the rural school I offered to take over for her for a week while she went on her honeymoon. While there, I met Mrs. Thompson, the Hot Springs County Superintendent of Schools. Later that year she remembered me when a teacher was needed for a rural school a few miles north of Allison's, and called to see if I'd be interested in taking it for the following year.

Frank and I talked it over at length. I would be over 100 miles from home, but when the fence building season was over there would be no reason why he could not spend time with me. The strong argument in favor of it was that it would give me more equity when I was eligible for Social Security. I could not draw benefits from working for my husband. So I called Mrs. Thompson and told her I would take it.

There was a completely furnished teacherage next to the schoolhouse. All I needed to take was bedding, linens, groceries and clothes. I was surprised to find that all 13 students were girls. Among the highlights of this interesting year were visits from Santa Claus and some state school officials.

A friend of mine who had also grown up in Buffalo was now married to an executive at the Hamilton Dome oil field southwest of our school. On one visit I half-jokingly said to Pete, "Why don't you come over and play Santa Claus for our Christmas program?" He took me up on it immediately and said he had been the official St. Nick at Midwest for years, and still had his costume.

The girls kept asking who was going to be Santa Claus, to which I responded that we were going to have the *real* thing this year. Their curiosity was building as inquiries disclosed that no local person had been contacted to fill the part. Pete didn't come over to the school until it was time for his appearance, and then came bursting through the door with a boisterous greeting. No cotton beard or cheap suit - he was perfect.

Our other visitor was the State Superintendent of Schools and two other state officials, who were making a survey of some of the rural schools. The state "super" seemed well impressed by the morning spent with our class, and then the group was invited to lunch at a large ranch owned by Brownie Bell Merrill McGee. She told me she planned to show these people from Cheyenne that we were not completely ignorant of social amenities - even though we lived out in the boondocks. She had her daughter and another woman don maid uniforms and serve an elegant four course meal - I'm sure these school officials were impressed with the fringe benefits of their visit.

Some of my students lived about four miles from school where their parents had jobs working on Anchor Dam. I had visited this government-financed project and met the geologist, who told me that he had determined that the formation and soil were not good for building a water tight dam. Despite this negative report from their own geologist, the government engineers had orders to build the dam anyway. Millions was spent. Then the day came to turn Owl Creek into the construction, and it was discovered that the dam would not hold water. Since 1961 when the project was completed there have been many unsuccessful attempts to seal it, but it is still dry.

We ended the year at Anchor School with an end-of-the-year tea party at the school house. The girls had fun decorating open-faced sandwiches and we had a lace cloth for the table, silver coffee and tea service, and pretty dishes. I gave the girls lessons in serving the tea and coffee, and they all took turns "pouring." The afternoon was a great success with all the ladies wearing their best clothes, hats and gloves.

The school district wanted me to sign a contract for the next year, but although I enjoyed the teaching job it was too far from home.

In the early fall of 1961 I had a call from the Ten Sleep School asking me to come over for a conference. It seemed they needed a teacher for the Nowood school, a rural school near the Woods ranch 30 miles south of town. It sounded interesting, and since Frank was doing a good deal of fencing at that time and was gone during the week, it seemed a propitious time to add to my earnings.

The three years spent at the Nowood School were delightful ones. I had eight girls and one boy. One of the girls, Chris Smith, was my only eighth grader. She was at least three years older than the other students, and I am sure she must have been bored by all those juniors. She probably thought, "My what a bunch of ignoramuses, I know they haven't the least idea what I am interested in." I felt sorry for her as I thought she should be with her peers. All the others were near enough the same age to enjoy each other in their games and outdoor activities. Even Freddie joined in with enthusiasm, although no doubt he occasionally wished he could get away from all those females and get out with a bunch of boys.

The entire group was artistic, especially the Woods girls whose mother was a sculptor. Friday afternoon after recess we set aside for art. Those kids turned out examples that I was proud to display for visitors. We also had some unique programs during the year. While we were studying Wyoming history, we wrote a skit in which many early Wyoming historical characters were represented.

My apartment was a roomy, well-furnished structure attached to the school room. Between the two units was a hall and the girls' and boys' bathrooms. I had my own bathroom off the bedroom. My living room was a long room with a kitchenette in one end. George Woods, the girls' father, had the job of keeping our cistern full of water - no small task. We learned to be very economical with our water.

Rather than a County Superintendent as I had previously, we were supervised by the Ten Sleep Superintendent. He was most cooperative, and even sent out the band teacher to acquaint our student body with the intricacies of band instruments. Learning to play simple tunes on them was exciting for these kids.

This band teacher was a most unusual man. He was an Austrian who had lived in Minnesota for awhile before coming to Wyoming. He was still somewhat a stranger to American ways, and spoke with a marked accent. His manners and speech held the attention of these children of rather limited experiences. I learned later that he did not look forward to those 30 mile trips over narrow, unimproved roads with any degree of equanimity. In fact, one day when he didn't show up we were told that he had run off the road into a patch of very tall sagebrush. It shook him up a bit but he wasn't hurt.

The summer after my first year at the Nowood school I made arrangements to go to Billings, where I entered Eastern Montana State College in order to earn credits to maintain my teaching certificate. At first I was horrified to find that I was entered in the second year new math class when I hadn't had first year. The instructor, when I told her of my dilemma, very generously kept me "after school" a few afternoons and painstakingly went through the logic of the new method. It was logical and not hard to comprehend once one got through the basics.

The courses I took were all very interesting. Years ago, everything I took in college was a brand new topic to be learned from the ground up. Here I was adding immeasurable enrichment to subjects I had encountered frequently. I am convinced that experience sandwiched between college courses adds great value to the latter. I went back to Billings the following summer with the same positive results. Included in my courses was music appreciation which was taught by an alumnae of

Roosevelt University, formerly the Chicago Musical College, my old alma mater.

Our Christmas programs at the Nowood school were quite the social gatherings, and were enjoyed by all. The schoolhouse was bulging with people who came from miles around, bringing refreshments for the social hour that followed any kind of get-together in the country. I resurrected a hand-me-down tuxedo, borrowed a top hat from a Mason and, lo and behold, we had a very authentic reader of *Night Before Christmas* - the author, Clement C. Moore, himself (AKA Chris Smith). The rest of the students acted out the poem as it was read.

During the year we had a table upon which the children were building a panorama, which they were allowed to work on when they finished their assignments. The theme was an Indian village. Their teepees were of paper, and the horses were sculpted expertly from clay that needed no kiln.

At the end of three years I felt we had made real progress. The board asked me to take the school for the next year, but Frank and I had made a decision to go south for the winter, so I refused. The school was shut down and preparations made for the students to attend Ten Sleep Schools for the following year. I felt it was a good decision as none of the pupils had had contact for more than a day or two with other children, as far as a scholastic environment was concerned.

Later that summer of '65 I was visited by a couple of ladies married to the Orchard brothers, who lived several miles beyond the Nowood school. They wanted me to come out to the ranch and tutor their children for the coming school year. We had pretty well finalized our plans for going south, which I explained to them. Between them they had several boys who, from what I gathered, would have been a greater challenge than the group I had just left. I felt comfortable with my decision. Besides, it would have meant another session of summer school in Billings. Although this would have given me a degree, circumstances dictated our first decision.

The eight girls and one boy I had at the Woods school became very dear to me. I have managed to keep in contact with nearly all of them, as they occasionally come by for a visit. Those who attended Ten Sleep High were active in school affairs and popular with their new school mates.

Verna and students at the Nowood School

Chapter 14

Desert Winters

The following summer we started formulating plans to go south for the winter. To where, we didn't know, but avoiding the bitter cold and snow was our aim. Frank and I both felt that the warmer climes and lower elevation would alleviate his worsening breathing problems. Later, in Arizona, a doctor confirmed that the problem was emphysema, brought on, no doubt, by almost fifty years of smoking.

We drove over to Worland and found a camper trailer with a folding tent top and built-in bed with large storage space beneath. That seemed to be just what we needed. We packed it with bedding, a gas camp stove, camp dishes, staples, clothing, writing material and a few books. Late in the fall we took off for the sunny south with blithe spirits.

We had no specific destination, which we found to be a mistake. We just drove south. We were well into California before we decided to park our trailer and rest for a while, near the Mojave desert. That word to me

connoted dryness and warmth. The four or five days there
belied my conception of the desert completely. It was cold
and rained every day. The only heat we had was when we
turned on the gas stove to prepare a meal.

Fortunately we had a neighbor, an elderly man
who was traveling alone and lived in a comfortable
trailer. He wanted someone to talk to so had us over
several times during our short stay there. It was a good
trade, conversation for warmth. To our surprise we
greatly enjoyed his company as he was a serious student
of the Bible from a philosophical point of view. We had
some most interesting discussions before we found a day
clear enough to dry out our bedding and tent and be on
our way south looking for a warmer spot.

One day as I was wandering around the desert I
noticed a pile of brush that looked a little unnatural.
Upon investigating it I discovered it had been placed in
front of a cave opening. I was more curious than cautious,
so moved the brush and entered the cave. A paper plate
sat on the floor and beside it a half smoked cigar. At that
point I became a trifle uneasy and returned to camp to
report my findings.

We visited the site with some new-found friends
early the next morning. Our friends said no car had been
in the area since they moved in a week ago, so our
mystery man must be afoot. We were miles from any
habitation. Strange indeed! The authorities had had no
reports of escaped convicts, so our mystery was never
solved. We found that the desert contains many such
mysteries that added a certain aura to the place.

We enjoyed watching airplane maneuvers daily as
the plane "towed" a fake missile behind and other planes
would shoot at it. One day when the four of us were
hiking we came upon a two inch shell half buried in the
sand. That was when we made plans to move out of the

area which we learned later was a practice ground for war planes and taboo to citizens!

After several days of camping in the desert, we were becoming a little weary of this "back to nature" life and decided to look for more permanent lodgings. That was the end of our camping, and for the remainder of our five winter years in Arizona we rented, eventually finding a small house in Quartzite, Arizona.

The people we met were as interesting as the countryside. At one place our neighbors were a young Mexican couple, Mary and Pedro. She and I became good friends and made a trip to Mexico where she proved invaluable in bargaining with the Mexican shopkeepers, who find it highly entertaining and profitable to bargain with American tourists. This time, however, they found that Mary had the advantage, as she was on to their wiles.

Mary attempted to teach me a little conversational Spanish in return for a lesson in crocheting. I must say she was a better student than I was. When I asked her one day to "open the door" in Spanish, it came out, "open the pig!"

Judging by the elaborate album of wedding pictures I saw at their place, Mary and Pedro had a most sumptuous and expensive wedding that had to have cost more than he made in a couple of months at his job at the cotton gin. We were surprised to find such large cotton fields in California, having associated that business with the southeastern states.

We visited the gin one day, where truck load after truck load drove up to the building where the gin was located. With a huge vacuum Pedro unloaded the truck of loose cotton in minutes into the conveyor that led to the machine that removed the seeds and made it ready for the mill. When the cotton is all picked, the stubble is burned. When that conflagration swept across those huge fields, the smoke could be seen for miles. I am sure the air pollution was felt for miles, also. No doubt that situation has changed during the past 30 years.

On Christmas Day Frank and I packed a lunch and drove to the Salton Sea, a salt water phenomenon 236 feet below sea level. A nearby flag pole 236 feet tall showed where sea level would be. I felt a trifle uneasy to think that not too many miles away there was a terrific expanse of water, the Pacific Ocean, that much over my head! The water was crystal clear but entirely unpalatable. As we sat in the warm sun after lunch utterly relaxed, I wondered idly what the purpose might be of that myriad of tiny snail-like creatures that inhabited the brackish water at the water's edge, and how they had evolved from ancestors of a surely much more friendly environment.

We had some nice days in California but we prepared to move on east to Arizona which, from all reports, promised to be a drier climate than we had experienced so far. On our way out of the state we pulled onto a side road to visit an old abandoned gold mine that Frank had heard about. It was called the American Girl Gold Mine. We were surprised when we got there to find so much evidence still visible attesting to the expanse of the operation. There were large rock foundations left of what was apparently large stores, hotels and certainly a hospital, considering the concentration of remains of medicine bottles around the premises. I had a ball collecting purple glass, including one intact medicine bottle with 1870 stamped in the glass.

Frank was also looking for colors, not purple, but gold. He was panning some of the tailings from enormous piles left around the site. I think there had been too many before him with the same idea, for he never did come up with anything of any consequence. However we didn't leave the place empty handed. We stopped at a rock shop and bought a handful of beautiful polished stones, agates, tiger eyes, and turquoise. I had them around for years, finally having some set as pendants for Dorothy, Allison and myself and one in a belt buckle for Jim, as mementos of our trip.

After leaving the gold mine we crossed the Colorado River, whose muddy waters slogged along like a tired old man worn out after such a long journey. I had a vision of this stream at its head in the Rockies. Rushing and leaping over the rocks, clear and unblemished as a healthy youth, then gathering pollution and silt from other rivers and drainages along the way, until at last it rolls laboriously along and meets its demise in the ocean.

Quartzite. Aha! Quartz - a magic word for geologists. The name alone was enticing and the town looked as if it had possibilities.

We were quite comfortable in Quartzite and enjoyed prowling in the desert. I had always thought of the desert as a vast expanse of sand with no vegetation except near oases. The desert floor in this area was composed of very smooth pebbles set close together in the sand with a fairly firm surface, creating a beautiful mosaic effect. The surface seemed to have acquired a sort of patina that gave it the appearance of expensive leather.

Dry washes were the main roads for "desert rats" who carried "tracks'" of carpet or wire mesh which they unrolled and placed ahead of the wheels to provide traction where the sand was treacherously soft. These washes that looked like old river beds were deceiving. After a sudden heavy rain they would be almost bank full of muddy, rushing water for a short while. It was enough to keep the trees growing.

The trees are not of great size, such as the ancient oak and maple trees of Texas, or the huge old cottonwoods we have in Wyoming. The mesquite is noted for its vicious thorns. It, along with the palo verde, has small narrow leaves to prevent loss of moisture through evaporation. The palo verde is the state tree. In the spring it is covered with yellow blossoms so thick that at a distance it resembles a giant chrysanthemum.

The general contour and denseness of the smoke tree with its myriad of tiny smoke colored leaves resembles a puff of smoke when seen from a distance. We brought one in one day and used it for a Christmas tree. We were delighted with the results after adding some decorations.

It was such a great feeling to be able to spend so much time out of doors. When it rained it poured for a short while then it was all over. The sun would pop out again and we were ready to hike out and observe the transformation of the desert. It would be ablaze with red and yellow flowers as if a giant magic wand had swept over the land, awakening the flowers that had lain dormant since the last big rain.

Many of the temporary residents of Quartzite were rock hounds. They would leave every morning in groups, returning in the evening with their coffee cans of specimens which they would compare with others' findings. I think they probably did some swapping if they had duplicates. Most of them were looking for something unusual to set on their mantle at home, or maybe use as a conversation piece door stop. We didn't join these excursions, as we would rather have a more quiet day while Frank studied the geology of the area.

We left for Wyoming fairly early in the spring after our first winter in the Southwest, feeling that this would be a good place to return to next year, with its uncluttered desert and uninhabited hills. We both enjoyed the warmer temperatures and the low altitude made breathing easier for Frank.

Spring in Wyoming is my favorite season. It is full of promises that we know will be fulfilled sooner or later. In the part of Arizona where we were, the seasons are not distinctly marked. The only difference between them is the temperature. Winter might bring just a little more rain, but rarely do the residents see a snowflake. One season slides into another with little notice.

On the other hand, there is nothing so thrilling as to observe the first harbingers of spring in Wyoming, although we know what to expect every year. We hear shouts of "Spring is here!" when the meadowlark announces it loud and clear from his perch on the sagebrush, or when we see the geese surveying the ground around the lake, or when we come upon the hardy little purple pasque flower poking its head up, even if it has to break through a layer of snow to do it. The velvety pussy willows tell us we may soon expect to see trees don their summer mantle.

As we neared home, these thoughts of spring gave me a sense of security. It was wonderful to be in our own comfortable house in Ten Sleep again, and we surely enjoyed the yard. We spent hours in our lawn chairs in the shade on our green lawn, and in the evening watched the night hawks zoom down to catch mosquitoes and the stars appear gradually in the sky. After enjoying our summers and falls in Wyoming, we would head back to Arizona before winter set in.

The clerk at the store in Quartzite not only sold her wares, but she served as a great catalyst in introducing the winter residents from all over the country to each other when they came in. It was thus that I met the superintendent of the Ehrenburg School, Mr. McElhaney, at the beginning of our second year there, and he said he had heard that I was a teacher. They needed a substitute teacher there for awhile, as the regular teacher was ill. I told him somewhat of my experiences and qualifications. He said he would let me know later. I found out "later" meant after he had talked it over with his wife, who proved to make the final decisions.

In the meantime, we talked it over at home and were ready with an affirmative answer when he came the next day and offered me the job. The McElhaneys came by for me Monday morning in their vintage Cadillac and drove down the freeway to the little village of Ehrenburg and beyond it a mile or two to the schoolhouse, a long, one story brick building containing four classrooms, an office and a storeroom for supplies. I had the fifth and sixth grades.

As I looked over my students they seemed like an average group, but I discovered little by little that they were a most unusual bunch of kids. Possibly a third of them came from normal two parent homes. The others were from homes with single parents, step parents, live-in mates, and so forth. Their former teacher, I discovered, had succumbed to a nervous breakdown. He never came back, but stole away silently, not to be heard from again.

My past years of teaching were no doubt a help, but I really had no great discipline problems, except for one boy who didn't accomplish anything all year. He could barely read to start with, was withdrawn, and very seldom finished an assignment. I never heard him make a spontaneous statement. I learned his father was abusive. He had one friend who talked to him so I let them study together, which brought a few positive results.

Benny was just the opposite. He talked all the time and was a leader. I noticed that at recess his playmates would group around him and wait for him to suggest what they should do, or what game to play.

Billy was the pampered child of a doting couple. He was lazy, having never had to do anything at home. After staying in at recess to do his lessons for a week or so, he improved his ways somewhat. His parents and one or two other families were the only ones who ever inquired about how their children were doing.

School activities were at a minimum. There were no organized games or programs at school. Since I could play the piano, I talked the other teachers into having a Christmas program, which was to be all singing. I was amazed at some of the talent that we uncovered during practice. They loved it and we had a good representation of parents at the program. It was the first time I had met most of them. Although this was a small community, people didn't gather and visit after the program as in Wyoming. The people in this community lived close together but were not neighbors.

Mrs. McElhaney, the principal's wife, was a righteous individual. She came into my room one day and gave a little talk to the kids about a new family who had just moved into town. She said, "They are very poor and bring real skimpy lunches. Now I know some of you have more than you can eat." She continued, "If you have untouched sandwiches or food that they could use, don't throw it away but give it to me and I shall see that these poor children have more to eat." With that she went out and my flock finished their lunches.

John, who always fixed his own lunches, and probably his breakfast and dinner too, always brought a can of Vienna sausages and a piece of bread for his lunch. He would eat about half of the meat and then toss the can into the garbage. After seeing him do the same on this day, I said, "John how about saving your sausages for the new kids?"

He replied, "Mrs. Davis, I went by their place last night and they were both sitting on the front step smoking cigarettes. If they can buy cigarettes, they can buy their own Vienna sausages!" I didn't pursue the matter any further.

Our classroom had an apparatus in the corner that was labeled "air conditioner," but all it did was make a terrific noise and blow dust around. Our apartment was also hot. We didn't get any relief at night, either, as we do in Wyoming. From June on we could expect temperatures between 70 and 80 at night.

A few of the pupils brought me little gifts on the last day of school. There were no picnics and no fare-thee-wells, but at the stroke of one o'clock the McElhaneys were out the door and loading their Cadillac for the last trip to Quartzite. They had not been rehired for the following year, and were going to have to test their evangelical proclivities elsewhere. As for the students, their future seemed as bleak as the wind swept desert.

I was called to substitute several times during the following year. The new principal (who although he was the head man at the school hardly deserved the title of superintendent) held sway at a small office where he sat at a little desk surrounded by stacks of supplies: paper, pencils, crayons, books, etc. I went in one day to get some drawing paper for an art class. He was sipping something from a coffee cup. He offered me a drink and said, "This is the only way I can get through the day." I felt it was difficult enough to manage with all my faculties. I doubted very much if it would help matters any by trying to obliterate the problem.

As usual we were eager to get on our way north. We felt a little like a horse who had been tied to the hitching rail for hours, and when untethered heads for his green pasture and a shady spot along a cool stream.

Visits from our three children were happy occasions we could always expect during the summer in Wyoming. Dorothy and Dick lived nearby with their interesting family of five girls and one boy, all very competent in the house or in the field or on horseback, riding the hills.

Jim, a geologist with Union Pacific Resources in their office in Laramie, his wife Dorothy Ann, and their two girls were always welcome. Jim and his dad could talk rocks in much more technical terms than we ever heard from the rock hounds in Arizona. Jim's forte was uranium mining and exploration. This was a hot item at the time. Allison, Keith and their three children, Jody, Karla and Tyler traveled over from Lander. We visited my mother in Buffalo when possible.

The summer passed all too quickly, and in November we made preparations to go south again. It was a great feeling to drive up to last year's dwelling and unpack. No searching for a house this time.

Frank and I continued to spend lots of time in the desert and never ceased to be amazed at the wonders of this vast natural museum. I found the saguaro most interesting. It is an enormous cactus that can swell to a foot in diameter after a rain, and can grow to be 50 feet tall. The stem is the fleshy part of the cactus, and the thorns are the leaves. The bloom of the saguaro is a huge white flower appearing at the top of the plant. All one sees from the ground is a little bit of white at the edge. The branches or arms of this plant bend upward. All similar yet all different. When I first beheld a group of these odd cacti I felt as if I were in the presence of a congregation of somber men raising their arms in agreement, or maybe protest, while the barrel cactus and the prickly pear stood mutely by.

The "jumping cactus" seemed capable of attaching its thorns to my socks from some distance away. Except for some of the flowers, almost all of the desert plants seemed to have thorns. There is a common saying here, "If it grows, it's thorny ,and if it moves, it bites!"

The creosote bush is unfriendly in a different way, exuding a sap that smells like creosote and polluting the ground around it so that nothing else will grow.

We made an excursion to Crystal Mountain one day. It was just what its name implies. Lying on the barren surface of the hill were beautiful quartz crystals. If you were really lucky you might pick up one that was a perfect prism.

At that time there seemed to be no restrictions against carrying off samples. Ditches had been chiseled into the side of the hill, evidence of rock hunters in search of bigger and better specimens. A friend told me years later that the entire mountain had been devastated, with an unbelievable share of it being carried away.

One spring we went home by way of the Grand Canyon. No picture in a magazine or on TV, or no description by the most graphic writer will prepare the first time visitor for the mighty scale of this natural wonder; miles wide and over 6000 feet deep in places. We are used to seeing things a mile away on the surface of the earth, but to look almost straight down a mile and see a river is awesome indeed.

In Navajo country we saw numerous Navajo hogans - domed structures made of mud, held together by branches and covered with mud or sod for insulation from the heat. The small entrance always faces east. Each hogan had its own clay oven outside the dwelling.

There weren't many automobiles, but we saw many couples and families walking. As we left the village and drove towards the next town, miles away, we spied two little specks in the far distance, which proved to be an elderly couple hiking along the hot road. She had on a beautiful embroidered shawl, even though it was a hot day. We offered them a ride which they accepted with beaming faces, expressing their appreciation more than their meager English vocabulary could. We parted company at the next town and went on our way north.

In early November of 1968, before we set off for Arizona again, we made a trip over the mountains to see my mother, who was almost 90 years old and had not been in the best of health. I found her very weak and tired. It was so hard to leave her, but my brother Bear was living with her, and along with Ralph and Dick, who lived in Buffalo, she was well looked after. Nevertheless it was very hard to leave and know we would be gone for so long. Frank would have difficulty fending for himself, at this point, and there was no one but me to look after his needs.

We left Buffalo mid-afternoon. For the next couple of days we were busy making final preparations for our departure. We had disconnected our phone for the vacation, so I went next door to give Dorothy a last call before leaving. I picked up the phone and someone was dialing on the other end. I said hello and discovered it was Dorothy, trying to reach me. She said, "Grandmother died last night in her sleep." Somehow I was not as shocked as I might have been had I not seen her so recently.

The family all met in Buffalo. It was good to see my brothers Lawrence from Denver, Leland from Richland, Washington as well as the three from Buffalo. Melvin had died the previous year. We relived those happy times of our uncomplicated childhood, and reflected on how we were all made to feel the importance of learning and knowing about the world around us by Mother's example. She was an avid learner until the day she died.

Soon afterwards Frank and I were ready to go south again. At least we didn't have to worry about looking for a house when we got there, as we would move into the same place.

We had visitors every winter, including our three children, grandchildren and friends and relatives from many places. Viewing new sights and experiencing new activities is always exciting, but seeing familiar faces was a real comfort. We appreciated all of these visitors very much.

One day, while browsing through books at the mobile library van, I met a woman who seemed to have the same interest in literature as I. I looked forward to visiting with her every time the bookmobile came through.

One day she told me she had a large collection of *Arizona Highway* magazines. She offered them to me if I wanted to come over after them. That magazine is beautifully illustrated, and it would be wonderful to have a stack of them to browse through. I lost no time in driving over to her place.

The white adobe house was at the edge of town. Chimneys protruded everywhere, denoting lots of fireplaces. There was one in each of the three bedrooms as well as the kitchen and dining room. We went into one of the rooms where the magazines were. There they were, probably a hundred or more stacked on a shelf next to the fireplace. However when we drug out a pile of them shreds of paper fell all over; they were completely riddled by termites. Every page had trails left by the insects as they gnawed their way through. So much for my anticipated browsing!

We sat in the kitchen and talked for awhile. It was a cheery place, with hand-crocheted, brightly colored pot holders of every design and color hanging on the wall. At the side of the fireplace was a bunk bed occupied by her husband, who was semi-invalid. He too was quite erudite, and the three of us had some lively conversations.

I was surprised to learn that they had five children who, for the most part, had been educated at home and were now out on their own. It seems they all loved to travel and would pack up and take off to wherever their fancy led them. They weren't sure where the children all were, and stranger yet, something came up about birthdays and the mother made a startling announcement, "Oh dear, we never paid any attention to birthdays, we never had time and I don't remember when any of our birthdays are!" That is the first and last time I have ever heard such a statement from anyone!

Frank's breathing problems were getting worse and I had been more than a little concerned about the trip home, and so was greatly relieved when Jim called and suggested he assist us on the trip home. During these last few weeks in Arizona Frank was becoming more and more withdrawn and reluctant to converse with anyone but me.

This seemed quite natural as I could supply his needs that he was unable to provide for himself. At this point I was not planning ahead any further than the trip home.

The crest of the red hill just west of Ten Sleep presents a beautiful view: the alfalfa fields framed by red hills on one side and tree-lined Ten Sleep Creek on the other. North of the Creek sits the little village with its wealth of trees and neat houses. Not a junk yard in sight! It was doubly welcome to us, our silent thoughts in accordance, as we looked forward to opening our own gate, unlocking our own door, going in and sitting in our own chairs. Like a bucket of murky water which has settled leaving nice solid sand at the bottom and clear water covering it, we felt more settled and able to plan for the future from a more solid base.

On my first visit to the grocery store and post office my spirits were further boosted when everyone called me by my first name and people I met stopped to ask me about our winter.

I was anxious to hear from our daughter Dorothy, who was expecting her seventh child. They lived on a ranch about 14 miles from town, the last two miles of which were not surfaced but merely graded - which didn't help much when a heavy rain transformed that dirt road into a soggy mess. A telephone call assured us that everything was fine up there, and the weather was beautiful so far.

The week of April 20th saw a change in the weather which had us all concerned. Clouds and rain and more rain. Finally I got the long-awaited phone call. It was my son-in-law, Dick, "Well, Grandma Verna, you have a new grandson!"

"Oh," I said with relief, "you made it to the hospital!"

"Not all the way, but we are here in town at Kildow's, and everything is fine." This was after nine o'clock at night, so I would have to postpone my visit as I was sure Dorothy was ready for a rest.

Dick said that he was taking her on to Worland that night to have the doctor check her and the baby. She spent the night there and I wasn't too surprised to see them all drive in to our place the next day bright and chipper as could be. What an improvement over the '30s when they made invalids of us new mothers for ten days.

I heard the story of their trip then. They had started out at the first signs, with which they were both familiar. By the time they slogged through the mud and over the ruts and were out on the highway, Dorothy decided they had better stop in Ten Sleep. She fortunately remembered that the Methodists minister's wife was an RN, so to their house they went.

Reverend Kildow as well as Esther his wife were used to all kinds of exigencies, but this called for more than ordinary resourcefulness. They chose the bathroom as the delivery room. Doctor-Nurse Kildow soon had things under control and everything went with no complications. Dick and Reverend Kildow sat in the kitchen drinking coffee and I'm sure each was offering a fervent entreaty to the Almighty on behalf of his respective spouse. Dorothy was never admitted to the hospital or had a doctor during the delivery, saving enough money to buy a dishwasher!

We were close enough so that we saw the new baby Tim almost every week. It is always such fun to watch the development of a baby. It was a most welcome diversion that summer.

Frequent visits from the children lightened up our days as spring moved into summer. However Frank's health did not improve; breathing became more difficult and the least activity exhausted him. It is hard to see someone who had been so active and knowledgeable in so many fields lose interest in everything he did. I often found myself thinking back to the hours he spent in his shop during the winter months, inventing, building or repairing machines.

He had designed and built a small blast furnace capable of producing terrific heat, in which he melted down aluminum, poured it into square molds, then carved out a model of a car engine on the lathe with an unconventional offset cam. A similar design was produced by others later, and used in a car manufacturer's engine.

While we were fencing he designed a measuring device that contained four three inch bolts 8 or 10 inches apart. We would roll out our four strands of barbed wire then plant the rod next to the fence post, place the four wires over the bolts, and presto, they were ready to staple to the post in one operation instead of four. While we were on the ranch he designed a different dehorner that had more leverage than those on the market, thereby making the dehorning of larger horns much easier.

We had a creditable library containing many classics and technical books. These he no longer took down from the shelves.

If we had had the equipment that today's emphysema victims have, he could have been made more comfortable. As it was, his occasional whiffs from the oxygen bottle through an inadequate filter were not enough, and at this point the emphysema was calling the shots.

The end of his suffering came in mid-July, when he died at home. I was alone, but my dear neighbors came immediately to my assistance and were a great help.

The arrival of our three children lightened my load tremendously. They took over, and their alacrity at formulating and activating plans had us ready to go to Buffalo the next day. Frank was born in Buffalo in 1900 and 70 years later was being returned there to his final resting place beside his parents, Henry Winter and Annie Painter Davis.

On the way home I had plenty of time to reflect on the past 40 years, many good ones and some less so. But reflections of the past are smoothed out by time, just as reflections in the water are softened, thus making the reflection more beautiful than the real thing.

The children were of course loathe to leave, but I was determined to get at my problems and face up to those inescapable duties that only I could perform. I never did like the feeling of dread, and have found that only action will banish it. That was the route I chose.

Frank in the Desert

Chapter 15

Rebuilding

After I had sorted things out in the house, the shop and the yard, I found that I had a whole collection of things that I had absolutely no use for. When my children visited me I took the opportunity to bestow upon them any tools they needed. The remainder we decided to sell at a garage sale. This included a truck, a tractor, a lathe, wrenches, pulleys, nails, and many Model A Ford parts that I found in the attic of the shop.

I advertised in a few newspapers and granddaughters Gail, 13 years old and Amy, nine, came to stay for a week and help with the sale.

People arrived from all over on the day of the sale. The truck, tractor and lathe, along with fencing tools went immediately. Among the people I didn't know was a black man, well dressed and with a determined air about him. I learned he was president of the classic car club in Casper and was looking for certain antique car parts. I had a few things he wanted and he surprised me further by telling me I was not charging enough for my Model A parts. He very kindly assisted me in re-pricing them and gave me a $50 bill to pay for his purchases.

I had gone into the house for something when Gail came in and said, "Grandma, there's a kind of scroungy looking man out there looking at things. He has a beard and kind of long hair. I think maybe you'd better come out. While you talk to him I'll go out and get his license number."

I did as she suggested and she hadn't exaggerated in her description of him. He was closely examining the Model A parts that were left. As soon as he opened his mouth, I knew we had nothing to worry about, for he spoke like a college professor. Not surprisingly, I soon learned he *was* one, from Kansas State. While he was occupied Gail had a chance to tell me his car had a Kansas license plate. It all tied together except for one thing - how did he learn about the sale? "Well," he said, "I was spending some time at my mother's cabin in the Big Horns when I happened to see your ad in the Buffalo Bulletin." He took what was left of the car parts and happily went on his way.

We took in several hundred dollars. With additional money from the sale of the truck and tractor I felt not only rich, but expansive. I wanted to do something, take on a project that would involve some sort of change. Lately, my life had been like a long uphill road with no side roads to break the monotony.

The first idea that came to me was to make my little dwelling more livable, which I expressed to my brothers on their next visit. Ralph and Dick were gung-ho about the idea. They would help me in many ways, and as Bear was unemployed they were sure he could help with the construction.

The activities that followed would bring anybody out of the doldrums. Plans were drawn and redrawn, cement blocks and lumber were ordered. We found doors, rugs, hardware and windows at bargain prices. We got that extra bit of help from the lumber man in Worland and members of the family all came around to help at different points of the construction. By the next spring I had dramatically modernized my little house with a nice living room, new bathroom, and big windows looking out on the yard and the distant red bluffs by Ten Sleep Creek.

Ten Sleep house after remodeling

The construction project was still in progress when, in early September, I had a call from the Ten Sleep School Superintendent advising me of an opening as study hall supervisor. He wondered if I would consider it. So I went to work again.

This idea of a study hall was not a very successful program if it was supposed to entail what its name implied. Anyone who has ever had experience in the classroom knows that an idle student is not a quiet student. I struggled with this situation until the end of the first semester when the schedule was changed and I taught the typewriting classes plus social studies to the second grade. The latter was a delight. One little boy said, "Mrs. Davis, you make it fun!" That sort of accolade makes teaching rewarding.

By spring my house was pretty well finished. My teaching , or rather supervising, job was also finished. I was almost 70 years old. Supreme court justices and other professional people hold sway effectively way beyond that age, but handling kids required one of more sturdy build and preferably pugilistic training than I possessed. As for my house, the finishing of it meant the beginning of a much more comfortable life.

One of my friends who was a tremendous help in my rehabilitation was Ann Brown. She had supervised art in the Worland schools for years. Her husband Rap, a life long friend of the Burger family, had died suddenly of a heart attack two years previously. It was the following year that Frank died, so Ann and I found great solace in each other's company.

Ann encouraged me to start doing artwork again. I had taken a few lessons when we were in Arizona, but had not opened my paint box for years.

I had a pine slab fence around my backyard. A slab is the outside cut of the log, the bark is left on which makes a nice looking rustic fence. After removing the fence, I had piles of these slabs and could see no immediate use except for firewood. Ann and I put our heads together and decided they would make good painting surfaces.

Peeling off the dried bark revealed convoluted carpenter ant burrows. Short pieces of this "wormwood" provided an interesting background for my still life paintings of fruit or vegetables. A hanger on the back and they were finished. I could lose myself for hours with my paints and boards in front of me. It wasn't long before I had quite a collection. Ann took some to Worland and they proved quite popular.

In the meantime, I had received letters from Elsie Clements Lukas, my Chicago friend from music school days. She had lost her husband and wanted me to come visit her. The idea of visiting Chicago again was very appealing, however I didn't really see how I could finance a trip. I told her what I had been doing in my spare time and jokingly said, "Elsie, when I sell enough plaques to buy a plane ticket, I shall be on my way." Surprisingly I did, and late that summer found me on my way to the Windy City.

We saw the sights of Chicago using taxis, the buses, the 'L', the new subway (my first trip underground), and when possible in her son Luke's Cadillac.

At a science center there were models of everything, from a western cattle ranch with its fences, cowboys, cattle and corrals, to an atomic plant. There were demonstrations of gravity, levers and simple machines and geologic specimens.

A dinner at a log restaurant set in a grove of pine trees made me think I had been transported back to Story, Wyoming beside the Big Horn Mountains. Just to broaden our experience, Elsie's male hairdresser took us to a smoky beer pub for dinner.

All in all, my "art financed" trip was a delightful one. But it was with happy anticipation that I boarded the plane at O'Hare to return to the "Wild West."

Later that fall I discovered a lump in my breast which, following a biopsy in Casper, proved to be cancer. I was scheduled for immediate surgery.

My surgeon, besides being an expert in this particular field, was also a very compassionate man. He took time to explain everything to my children, easing their minds considerably, I am sure.

Recuperating in Ten Sleep, my next door neighbor Bertha looked in on me everyday, doing little thoughtful things until I insisted I should be able to take care of myself. But how easy it is to become accustomed to being waited on! I was reluctant to get at the housekeeping duties that confronted me. It was nice to sit in my easy chair and do nothing, but my private little Jiminy Cricket kept hounding me to get with it. I had my strength and ambition back before long and was pretty much back to normal in a few weeks.

*   *   *

Dorothy and Dick Redland had been in partnership on a ranching operation south of Ten Sleep on Spring Creek. They were beginning to feel somewhat inhibited there, and found it difficult to make any progressive changes. They began to explore new possibilities.

About the only way a rancher can operate is either by taking over an operation already in the family or on rare occasions find one for sale that he can afford to buy. They stopped by one day in the early spring of 1971, all agog with excitement over a ranch they had looked at in Fremont County, about 150 miles from Ten Sleep. If they could manage the deal, it would provide them with more acreage and a better location geographically. They were able to find a partner and the purchase of the ranch went through. I volunteered to find a place for them to store their furniture until their move in the fall.

I was told of a gentleman who lived a mile or two out of town whose wife had just passed away, and they thought   he was planning on going to California. That next weekend Jim and Dorothy Ann were here, so I suggested that we drive up and interview this man who just might have a room or a shed to use for storage. We drove up Ten Sleep Creek to his place, which I had known years before, but when we arrived I found nothing familiar. All of the old buildings had been torn down and replaced with a new house and garage.   It had a very neat, beautiful yard.

We were greeted by Ken, the owner, whose urbane manner caught us rather by surprise. I explained my dilemma. During our visit we learned that he spent winters at his home in Santa Barbara, California and left everything at his Wyoming cottage ready to come back to in the spring. He happened to remember, however, that his neighbors were moving into a new house and perhaps their old one might be available for storage.

As we left Ken's neat little place on the bank of the Creek we pondered why someone with his background would buy land and build a house in this remote area. We drove on over to the place as we had been directed and found what we were looking for.

The following week I had a phone call from Ken asking if I could use some apples. "Of course, I would love some!" He was down the next day with the fruit and stayed for a most edifying visit. We discovered we had both attended Northwestern University, and also that his father was a cement contractor in Chicago; my dad was the same in Buffalo. It was interesting to find he had two girls and one boy, same as I.

The following week brought an invitation from him to ride to Lander for the day. It was a most enjoyable trip. We found that our taste in music was also similar, and listened to classical music for the entire trip. As he recounted some of his experiences, I was beginning to understand the apparent incongruity between his rather cosmopolitan life and his simple lifestyle in Ten Sleep.

He went from life in the city to a ranch in western Colorado, thence to some acreage near Lander where he retired, hoping his wife's health would improve. She was also a victim of emphysema. They had visited Ten Sleep or at least passed through a few times. Mrs. H. fell in love with the place, so that is where they finally moved, and where she died. He kept the place as sort of a summer retreat from the hustle and bustle of California living. He wondered at the same time what held me in this small village where, as he expressed it, "The only cultural event of the year is baccalaureate!"

This was the beginning of a long and wonderful friendship. We both enjoyed touring around aimlessly over the mountains. I learned that his love of the Big Horns was what brought him back to this country every spring when he knew the meadowlarks would be singing.

With no destination in mind we took countless trips that provided us with a wealth of new and exciting vistas. I had always had a yen to explore side roads, but until now the only ones we had ventured onto were those that had a job waiting at the other end, and a lot of those inviting glens or interesting rocky slopes had been viewed only from a moving vehicle.

Now that we were both retired from work but not from seeking adventure, we were finding time to appreciate the lovely mountain meadows with their profusion of wildflowers. The little mountain streams with their soothing, rippling music can obliterate all care if listened to quietly.

We took off one day intending to cross the south end of the Big Horns on a dirt road we thought would take us to Kaycee - a 70 mile trip. Instead, we drove for miles over a precipitous and narrow mountain road that took us out onto the foothills, where the road became even more risky, as it followed the ridges and avoided the draws, as no doubt they would be impassable in wet weather. We had been on the road for hours and had only a general idea of where we were. It was a most welcome sight to spot the blacktop highway to the east of us a mile or so away, and with a great sigh of relief we pulled onto the highway and headed in the general direction of Buffalo. We reached a restaurant some six hours and over 200 miles after we had left Ten Sleep.

Kenneth stayed until November that year, giving us a golden opportunity to view the extravaganza that the fall colors provide on the mountains, as well as along the lowland rivers. For the first time I saw Shell Canyon from a highway that is indeed an engineering marvel, with its immense slabs of concrete supporting the highway, which is constructed close to the canyon wall. We reached the noted Shell Falls and climbed down steep steps to reach a platform from which one is rewarded with a magnificent view of the falls crashing over the rocky ledge to the stream below. In recent years a lovely trail has been constructed, presenting picturesque views of smaller falls, interesting formations and plaques identifying various shrubs and trees that grow along the way.

On the pass at Burgess Junction we passed by a meadow solid blue with lupine. This highway has its own distinctive treat for each season of the year, but in the autumn, the aspens' brilliant orange and yellow and occasional deep red of the smaller shrubs against the deep green of the spruce and pine gave us a view that is not easily surpassed by any other season of the year.

I was sorry to see my new found friend leave, but we both knew that winter would soon be showing its hoary head and unpredictable habits, and travel might become hazardous. His parting injunction was, "Be sure and let me know if you make it to California."

During this busy summer there was action on other fronts as well. When school started in September the Redland children, Tom, Debbie, Della and Deena moved into town and stayed with me in order to start school. Deanna was then in college. They were there several days while their parents were moving stock and furniture to their new home on the Twin Creeks Ranch near Lander.

The final moving day arrived, and we loaded my car with clothes and suitcases and took off for Lander. It was snowing when we got there, and the furniture was being unloaded from the truck. By the time everyone made a dozen trips from vehicle to house through wet leaves and snow, the floors were pretty sad looking. I felt sorry for Dorothy, she had moved so many times. But she was never in any place very long before she was out shopping for material, wallpaper, paint or whatever she needed to satisfy her artistic and decorative needs. She couldn't wait to make a place look better than when she moved into it.

The house and yard were homey looking. There were lots of big trees in the yard and the creek ran near the house.

The second spring they were there, Danielle, who was barely four, and Tim, who was barely two, were playing in the sand near the creek while Dorothy was in the house. Dorothy was startled out of her wits when she saw Danielle try to open the gate, and when she couldn't get it open climb over the five foot wire fence and come racing to the house. Dorothy met her at the door and heard, "Mom, Tim is in the water and I can't reach him!"

Dorothy was out there in a flash and there was tiny Tim, in water up to his chest clinging for dear life to a willow sticking up out of the water. Dorothy rescued him in a jiffy. That incident taught those little tots more than a week of lectures could have. They gave that creek a wide berth from then on.

I missed my grandchildren after they moved to Lander, and was glad to get a piano class started. That year I had a most interesting group. There were several from high school, which is always a challenge. The band teacher, Kathy, also had a class of piano students. We agreed to put on a joint piano recital in the spring.

My friend Mary had taken many dance classes and since she had just returned from a sojourn in Hawaii, I approached her about working up some Hawaiian numbers for our recital. We had a grand production. The auditorium was packed and Mary's girls put on a super performance of Hawaiian dances with bamboo sticks. They danced over and between the long sticks which are manipulated rhythmically by a girl at each end.

During a trip to visit relatives in southern California I wrote Kenneth at his home in Santa Barbara to tell him I would be in nearby Ventura, the retirement home of Dick Redland's mother.

There was a letter waiting for me there from Ken saying that he would pick me up the next day. However our hosts had planned an excursion to Magic Mountain, so Dick and Dorothy would take me to Santa Barbara the following day. I recall less detail about Magic Mountain with its imitation scenery than I do of the mountain at my grandmother's where I hiked around 80 years ago. Magic Mountain depends upon man for its changes, whereas our real mountain depends upon nature, whose ways are surprising, rewarding, and sometimes mysterious.

It was not a very long drive from Ventura to Santa Barbara, but it was a pleasant one with lovely scenery all the way. Ken's house was an attractive southwestern style house on a large lot with lots of palm trees.

The interior spoke of his tastes in western things with furniture, rugs, and pictures. A Remington book lay on the coffee table. He had lunch ready for us, after which my folks returned to Ventura.

Kenneth showed me to an attractive little guest house across the driveway from the main house, where I was glad to snatch a few winks and relax in the quiet surroundings.

We spent the rest of the afternoon touring the city, a very pretty place. We were in one store I remember especially, a large emporium that contained only kitchen wares. One would need a degree in engineering in order to operate some of them!

The show place that impressed me most was the courthouse. As we entered the enormous front door we saw a staircase made entirely of brilliantly colored ceramic tile. Upstairs was the courtroom; what an austere place! Paradoxically it was luxurious at the same time. The dark wood paneling was beautiful, the molding artistically curved. The black leather upholstered furniture as well as the severe lines of the judge's bench added to the serious atmosphere. It couldn't have been more awesome had a stern judge and twelve somber jurors been sitting there waiting to hear our case. It was a relief to walk down those gaily colored stairs and out into the sunshine.

Kenneth suggested we drive down to Los Angeles and try our luck at the music center where the Nutcracker Suite was playing. We were not in luck this time as they ran out of seats just 15 people ahead of us.

No scalpers could be found, so we settled for a nice dinner at a restaurant under the same roof.

The entrance to the theater was lovely. I have never seen such massive and gorgeous chandeliers. The drive back to Santa Barbara on Highway 101 with the full moon shining on the ocean surpassed anything man could have produced, on stage or off.

After such a lovely evening I was definitely in the mood for our next day's trip which took us to the historic Santa Barbara Mission, which still contains some of the original crude furnishings and picturesque wall coverings. One half-expected a wizened little monk to rise from his cot in the corner and come forward to greet us.

At last it was time to leave Santa Barbara where the wondrous old mission contrasted with the modern examples of construction at the theater and civic buildings in Los Angeles; both overshadowed by the wonders of nature as we drove along the Pacific shore with the moon over the ocean. I was soon on my way back to Wyoming and more familiar living patterns.

Chapter 16

An Eastern Visit

During the summer of 1976 Ann Brown and I were getting together for trips to Buffalo where we both had relatives, or maybe just for a cruise around the Big Horns with our cameras, always on the lookout for a scene that might make a good painting.

During one of our excursions we decided it would be fun to take a trip to New York and Washington D.C. I had cousins in upstate New York and Ann's sister-in-law Frances lived in the Capital. We got down to business and had all the necessary preparations made and were ready to go by early October.

During our four days in Washington, Ann and I would rise early, fix toast and coffee (Frances was a night person and didn't get up until noon), and then call a cab to take us downtown and deposit us near whatever area we wished to explore.

My favorite display was the Air and Space Museum at the Smithsonian. I could have spent more than one day looking at those old planes that made history, like Lindbergh's Spirit of St. Louis, and the space capsule, which we could enter and see mannequins doing their thing while presumably shooting through space.

Ann preferred the art museums. We were fortunate to see some Calder mobiles in the sculpture collection that have become quite famous. We were tremendously impressed with the Kennedy Center, from the tall columns of water that shot up in the pond in front to the foyer, resplendent in its dimensions. It contained the tallest window that I have ever seen. The most unusual chandeliers were a gift of Belgium. Many pieces were gifts from other countries. The furnishings in all of the Capital buildings were luxurious, and authentic in design and style.

As tourists walked by the Lincoln Memorial it seemed conversation became hushed. There was something about that kind but rather sad face that seemed to be telling us something we needed to listen to carefully.

At the National Cemetery rows of white stone tombs were interspersed occasionally with a ponderous memorial monument, dedicated to specific heroes or causes. These contrasted sharply with the serene and simple Kennedy Memorial, with its eternal flame.

We were fortunate to be there during the changing of the guard, what precision! Those two handsome soldiers went through the rather long and complicated drill perfectly. It was thrilling to watch.

The many large memorial statues placed at intervals on the grounds were works of art and required more time to study than we could afford to spend at this time. We walked down the long avenue of fifty trees (A tree for each state in the Union with a plaque describing them) to get to our tour bus for the ride back to the city.

We had made arrangements to travel on Amtrak from Washington to New York, thinking we could see more than from a plane. In Wyoming one doesn't go very far on the highway without climbing a hill which of course gives the traveler an extended view. Not so in the East. There are very few hills from which to view the surrounding country. Furthermore, the tracks were lined with trees which restricted our sightseeing even further. We did come out in the open as we passed through Philadelphia, and were lucky enough to watch a fleet of sailing ships, part of the Bicentennial celebration. Their white sails gleamed in the sun as they sailed the Delaware River.

I was met at the New York station by my niece Susan. I had met Susan only a couple of times during her two brief visits to Wyoming. As a matter of fact, she was 40 years old before we were aware she was a member of the family.

It seems my brother and her mother had had a short affair which resulted in a pregnancy. My brother told me of it afterwards. She had returned to her home in Nebraska, my brother followed her and asked her to marry him but she wanted neither a husband nor a family. Susan was reared by a foster family who apparently had given her a good musical education. She had moved to New York to further her musical career which had been rather successful in Denver.

As Susan grew older, she wanted to know something of her parents. She knew her mother had been in Buffalo and knew what name to look for. She pursued this search and found the Burger name in the Buffalo, Wyoming phone directory at a New York public library. A phone call to her father was in turn followed by a visit from the long lost daughter herself. She was a charming young lady and a wonderful pianist and singer.

She seemed so glad to welcome a member of her family to her home, having been without a family connection for most of her life. We did enjoy visiting as we drove from New York City over those colorful New Jersey hills brilliant with red and orange foliage. As we drove through the small villages I was struck by all the little commercial signs in the yards or hanging from the front porches, advertising some sort of business, from sewing to dentistry, a New England custom.

We were greeted by her beautiful collie at her apartment situated in a large grove of birch trees, resplendent in their fall colors.

Susan's husband Tony was a chauffeur for a large chemical firm near their home. He got seats for Susan and me at a theater on 43rd Street in New York where we saw a great rendition of the show *Chicago*, with a wonderful cast. We took a cab afterwards to an Italian restaurant where Tony met us. After dinner we drove to Times Square.

I had always heard of that area as being connected to great festivities. It had deteriorated unbelievably. We stopped at a red light and immediately a disagreeable looking character came rushing up to Tony's car with a dirty rag. Tony quickly opened the window, handed him a coin and said, "Don't touch that windshield!" He explained to me that these panhandlers hope to get a little money for wiping windshields but do more harm than good.

As we sat there waiting for the light to change we saw hookers standing on the street presenting a startling degree of dishabille. The once famous but now infamous Times Square was depressing, so we did not tarry but went on past the United Nations, easily recognizable by its display of flags.

We took time to go up the Empire State Building, at that time the tallest building in the country. The elevator shot up to the top like a bullet. We didn't have much breath left to be taken away by that incredible view of the city. It was a clear night and the peaks and canyons made of brick, stone, steel and cement were an awesome sight from our high vantage point.

Tony's mother, sister and brother drove over from their home in Queensborough one afternoon. That was an interesting trio. The brother and sister, though middle-aged, were not married. There was no doubt, however, as to who the matriarch of that family was. I think she made Susan a bit nervous as she hovered over Tony, patting his knee and asking over and over, "Tony, are you all right? Aren't you thinner than you were? Are you working too hard?" She spoke with a strong Italian accent that gave her remarks a tone of solemnity.

When I expressed my appreciation of the delicious Italian pastries the Garrios had brought over for us, Madam Garrio said to her daughter, "You will send a box to Verna when she gets home." I explained to her the long tedious route those delicate pastries would have to travel to get to Ten Sleep, but she didn't seem to have a conception of distances and I don't think she understood the impossibility of such a venture.

The next day Susan drove me to Grand Central Station for the continuation of my trip to upstate New York. On the way we had a great view of the New Jersey hills. In Wyoming they would be sagebrush covered, but here they were a riot of color. Brilliant reds, yellows and greens, as if a giant tapestry had been thrown over the hills. Before long the harsh winds and storms of winter would rip that tapestry to shreds, leaving only the dull gray of the bare trees.

We reached Grand Central Station early and had breakfast there. We then descended to the nether regions of this gloomy place and waited for the huge steel gates to open that led to a rather awesome tunnel-like passage. I was struck by the unhappy expressions on everyone's faces, as if they were going down this tunnel to meet their doom. The trip to Syracuse along Chesapeake Bay was a memorable one, being more water than land.

I was curious to meet my cousin Dorothea, with whom I had corresponded since we were in high school. She and her husband were retired and I suspect they weren't too anxious to be disturbed out of their settled regimen. Nonetheless we took several trips around the area, seeing Theodore Roosevelt's summer home at the Finger Lakes, verdant misty valleys headed by majestic waterfalls, and the quaint old New England houses.

One of the daughters was the family genealogist so we spent one afternoon filling in gaps relative to the Wyoming branch of the family. Carleton, Dorothea's husband was a musician of sorts and I soon learned that his lifelong ambition was to produce a couple of fine musicians. I sensed that Carleton was a little disappointed that one daughter had gone into jazz, however the other daughter had devoted her life to classical music and had a large piano class in Syracuse. Music was almost their entire existence.

After my trip, it was almost the first of November and time to snuggle down in my little nest in Ten Sleep and prepare for the winter's activities: music lessons, substitute teaching, company, and a little bridge now and then if we could find eight people to get together at one time. I had always had a large list of correspondents and I could now bore them all with stories of that wonderful trip to the east coast.

Chapter 17

Texas Sojourn

Life is full of surprises. Some are fleeting, like seeing a bluebird on a fence post in the spring or looking out the window in time to see a gorgeous sunset just before it fades away. Some surprises are heard but not seen.

Dorothy and Dick called me one day from Lander with the announcement that they had put their ranch up for sale and were moving to Texas! Now this was a surprise with reverberations. It seems Dick had met a rancher from Texas who was spending the summer in Wyoming. He had glowing reports of the economics of running cattle in Texas, no feeding in sub-zero weather, no chopping water holes in the ice, and no government controlled pasture - all was privately owned and apparently not difficult to secure.

Dorothy and Dick went down to survey the situation and agreed on the move. I had no first-hand knowledge of Texas. I knew that it was a big state. A traveling cowboy who had worked down there on a ranch years ago told me he couldn't wait to get out, "Nothin' but wind, sand and scorpions," he said.

I had a dismal mental view of that state as being a vast, desolate plain with nothing to stop the wind, and very little water. Texas is an immense state, all right, but listening to a cowboy describe one little part of it is like two blind men examining an elephant. The man who felt the trunk said it's like a huge snake, while the man who passed his hands over the side of the animal said it's like a horse, only four times bigger.

So with Texas. Parts of West Texas would fit the description the cowboy gave, but I was to learn first hand much later that this state contains more contrasts in terrain, vegetation and climate than any other state I've visited.

Dorothy and her family moved down to Uvalde, Texas in the fall of 1977. She called me one evening all excited about an apartment she could get for me there. She was quite voluble as to the merits of Texas in general, and Uvalde in particular. My decision was really not hard to make as I had already decided to spend the winter months someplace where there was a warmer climate. It might as well be Texas. My daughter had been most enthusiastic about the positive features of this location.

I told her to take the apartment and I would be there in a couple of weeks. It didn't take long to make the necessary arrangements at the Worland travel bureau. Packing took me awhile as it was November and our weather was calling for warm coats and sweaters. But I had been assured that I would need nothing more than a light jacket or sweater - and no snow boots!

Uvalde is about 80 miles west of San Antonio. It was late evening, so I really didn't get a good look at the country we passed through. I had a feeling of excitement as we entered the town where I was to spend several weeks. It was bigger than I had expected. Main Street was brightly lit with attractive store windows.

The next morning I could hardly wait to get a better view of our surroundings. We went shopping for groceries and a few articles needed for simple housekeeping, then drove to my new quarters. I was not prepared for the beautiful mansion that was our destination.

On Mesquite Street there were three large houses on my side of the street. All sat back on their lots and were surrounded by huge oak and pecan trees. All had well kept grounds. At the end of the street was a large brick mansion which had been the home of Jack Garner, Vice President under Franklin Roosevelt. It had been made into an interesting museum.

The house in which my apartment was located contained three other apartments. The property was owned by a fairly young lady whose ownership was the result of a quirk of fate. This lady lived in the neighborhood and had a handicapped son for whom she was struggling to provide. The original owner of the huge house became acquainted with her, and being childless and a widow, had become attached to the crippled child. Upon the widow's death, the house and property were left to the boy, with the mother as guardian of the estate.

The small heir and his mother chose to remain in their small home and depended on Ruth, one of the tenants, to manage the apartments. That was lucky for me, as Ruth and I became good friends and she held the apartment open for me the next year.

About five o'clock that evening there was a tap at the door. It was Ruth with a steaming hot casserole for my dinner. The first thing she wanted to know was whether I played bridge. When I answered in the affirmative, that seemed to open the door to many activities. As a result I met many wonderful friends whom I enjoyed for the twelve seasons during my sojourn in Uvalde.

My third year there I found it necessary to find a new place of abode as the apartment house had sold and the new owners wanted more permanent tenants. Dorothy and I were at a quilting party one afternoon and learned of a little house in back of a large house on Cherry Street. We lost no time after the party to look into this possibility.

This quilting bee, by the way, was just one of the activities being put on in town by a very enthusiastic group of ladies who were raising money to restore the beautiful old opera house that had flourished in the early days of Uvalde. Their diligence paid off, and in a few years it was officially opened. During the years I was there I witnessed some excellent musical and theatrical productions in that luxurious theater.

We drove to the address given to us and found an attractive house with a flower box along the front porch and a cement block fence surrounding the place, along which bloomed a solid border of purple iris. A knock at the door brought a very pleasant elderly lady who was a little startled to see strangers on her doorstep. When we explained the purpose of our visit she invited us into her parlor which was obviously little used, with covers on the couch, organ and piano.

Grace seemed to be glad to have someone to talk to, and told us that her husband had been dead for several years. Before his death, but after he had retired, he would go out frequently on his boat - he was an avid fisherman. At this time when he was actively pursuing his pastime, she went into painting and had several examples of her art on the walls. Dorothy very adroitly remarked upon their merits and closely examined all of them, which I think won Grace over. She said she had never thought of renting her little house, she had built it for her studio, feeling she was entitled to spend as much on her hobby as her husband did on his.

It appeared that every time he bought something for his boat, she felt inclined to buy something for her studio. Grace went on to say that after the death of her husband she did not use the little house anymore. She had built a studio onto her house which was more convenient. She asked us if we would like to see the cottage, which of course we did as things were sounding encouraging.

When we walked into that attractive little cottage we couldn't believe our eyes. The floor and counters of the little kitchenette were tile. The cupboard contained dishes and pots and pans. There was a single studio bed, chiffonier, desk, end table and dinette set, all of maple. The small cottage, about 16 feet by 20 feet (perhaps a little larger than our Big Horn Mountain cabin) had seven windows plus a window in the door. There was a darling bathroom with white tile floor, pale turquoise tile walls and vanity top, and peach colored fixtures. She had really indulged herself when she furnished that little hideaway.

She offered it to me at a ridiculously low price. I think she was very lonesome and thought it might be nice to have someone close by. I lost no time in moving in. A serviceable cover for the bed, a couple of rugs for the floor, a table lamp and phone and I was all settled. The windows were all decorated with pretty yellow ruffled curtains. The big window over the sink looked out onto her lovely back yard where there were pecan trees, cypress trees and many beautiful flowerbeds containing roses, snapdragons and lots of ferns. I have never seen so many iris blooms; they bordered the entire yard, which must have been at least 100 by 200 feet. I felt as if I were in paradise.

In the spring when I was ready to return to Wyoming, Grace said, "Now I am not going to use that little house for anything. Just leave what you have in it and come back next fall." What good news that was, and to this cozy little nest I returned every year for eight years.

The time I spent in Texas provided an interlude in my life so vastly different from anything I had experienced. I could walk any day of the year with the assurance that I wouldn't encounter any ice or snow, and I was close to family.

Uvalde was once a very affluent town as evidenced by the beautiful architecture and the lovely big mansions and public buildings. The state in which these structures have been preserved speaks further of the citizens' pride in preserving their past. Houses were not crowded together as they are in some towns. One of the men who helped plan the town said he wanted the streets wide enough so that one could turn around on them with a four horse team. The population was consequently not compact.

A former governor was connected with one of the banks in town. His wife had toured extensively, collecting items for the bank including priceless rugs and pieces of antique furniture. Luxuriant, long velvet drapes hung at the tall windows of the lobby at the bank. There were four or five room-sized areas covered by authentic oriental or Persian rugs on which was placed a complete suite of antique furniture. Patrons were welcome to use these elegant settings for visiting or just waiting. This bank also contains a fabulous collection of original art by well known western artists. The place is on the must see list to show visitors.

I was spending a few days with my oldest granddaughter Deanna just for fun. Her friend, a lawyer who owned a plane, came up one evening and asked me if I would like to ride with him and Deanna to Dallas the next day to view the Ramses II exhibit. What a lark that would be! One sees a lot more from a small plane, as they fly lower than a jet. I was surprised at how comfortable the plane was.

The exhibit was a collection of the most beautiful objects one could ever imagine. This king was just a little boy when he assumed all of that power, but judging from all these elaborate possessions, most of them gifts, he must have been greatly admired (or feared).

We were a little late getting out of the exhibit hall and at the airport we had to wait quite awhile for clearance, then were directed through heavy air traffic entirely by the controller in the tower who referred to our craft as "Red Bird." Deanna had the flight map and by the instruments could tell about where we were. The voice from the tower was constantly giving directions. "Traffic coming in at 2 o'clock," meant a plane was approaching slightly to our right. We were a third of the way home before we could fly unobstructed in a straight line.

It was an indescribable sight as we flew over the many towns. From our vantage point they looked like so many diamond studded trinkets lying on the ground. I had visited Kerrville many times and was surprised to find it was a perfect horseshoe shape, outlined clearly by the lights. It had taken this shape as it was built along the river. What a sensation it gives one to get this very unusual perspective of places previously only viewed from the sidewalk. It is like comparing a bird's eye view to a worm's eye view.

Our pilot tells us as we approach the Uvalde airport that we have made a record run from Dallas due to a tail wind all the way. The rows of lights come on at runway number 5 and we make a perfect landing between them. After coming to a stop we taxi back to the hangar, alight, push the plane into its hanger and head for home.

Deanna's house was next to a large area of mesquite thicket. It evidently was a hiding place for illegal immigrants looking for work. The border patrol could be seen almost daily hovering over the brush-covered hillside in helicopters looking for them.

Many of these laborers would wander around the country looking for jobs. I had friends who hired some of them. It seemed rather harsh treatment to me, but these people slept in old sheds and were given only tortillas and a big pot of beans a day.

Long before I came to Texas I had heard that Kerrville was the place to go for art lovers. Dorothy had been there and vouched for that. I was ready to go. Our friend Wave, Dorothy and I departed one morning with light hearts and great expectations.   That was my personal attitude whenever I got into a car (or plane) in Uvalde, and I was seldom disappointed.

It was a beautiful day. Kerrville is about 80 miles north of Uvalde, and a little over 20 miles from town we enter the Hill Country, a large expanse of thickly wooded hills. The green foliage of the oak and mesquite and occasionally cedar interspersed with colorful mountain laurel, pink bud trees and wisteria vines make for slow traveling. Every bend in the road presents another beautiful bit of scenery that we wanted to capture on film. We stopped at Bandera, a small village on the edge of the Hill Country, for lunch. The weathered wooden building had a covered porch along the entire front. When we walked inside there was a row of cowboys perched on bar stools, complete in western gear. We thought for a moment that we had been transported to the town of Kaycee, Wyoming. The atmosphere was the same. We heard later that Bandera is noted for rodeos and dude ranches.

We walked down to the river and were rewarded with a most beautiful scene. The Medina River was a smooth, lazy flowing river lined with the most beautiful cypress trees. These trees grow at the edge of the water and the exposed, thick, entwined roots resemble the head of Medusa. The town was established by Mormons in 1852 as a cypress shingle camp. Many of the towns in Texas were dominated by certain ethnic groups. Bandera was principally Polish.

It is impossible to hurry through the Hill Country, there is so much to see, but we had only the afternoon left, so drove on to Kerrville. The main street is lined with attractive shops which consist of many kinds of craft shops, art galleries and dress shops. There were silver smiths, needlecrafts and decorations made of wood, tin or whatever. After a delightful afternoon of perusing the shops, we headed home.

One spring day I had a call from my friend Clara telling me she was contemplating a trip to east Texas to visit her old childhood home, her relatives, and to travel down the Azalea Trail. She asked if I would like to accompany her. She didn't have to ask twice; we made our preparations and were ready to go the latter part of March, a beautiful month in Texas.

The day we left was overcast with a mist in the air, occasionally condensing into rain drops.   But still the wildflowers along the highway, freshly washed by the rain, presented such vivid colors. These roadside flowers were a direct result of Lady Bird Johnson and her nationwide project to beautify the country.

We were soon going through a wooded area where I glimpsed my first dogwood trees. What a sight that was! These are actually more of a shrub than a tree, being much lower than the surrounding trees, but so very showy with their abundance of white blooms that showed up like lights on a Christmas tree. Not far from there we passed through a small village where dogwood was abundant and wisteria was draping its lavender mantle over any structure it could reach.

Big Sandy gave us a change of scenery. It is an old town established in 1877 where the Cotton Belt Railroad was built.   Here we saw some beautiful old homes with expansive grounds and colorful flower beds. I noticed the showy azaleas especially, as they are not common in Wyoming.   We saw ever so many bed and breakfast establishments that seemed to be doing a thriving business. I could see why - what a view to wake up to!

Our last stop was Hawkins, my companion's home town which had been an ordinary struggling community when she was growing up.   We drove around to some of Clara's favorite haunts, observing the tremendous change brought about by the discovery of oil.   Where once stood modest frame dwellings were now large brick homes surrounded by well kept grounds.   The churches were beautiful and the school buildings were modern brick structures with the latest in playground equipment in the school yards.   The school yards also had areas fenced off with high steel fences, inside of which were pumping oil wells.

We visited the cemetery where members of Clara's family were buried. No drilling was allowed inside the area which also was enclosed by an ornamental steel fence, however around the periphery were several producing wells. We learned that everyone who owned lots there was assured of perpetual care. Of course the streets and roads in the area were all in tip top shape.

As we had driven around this small town of just over 1,000 population, I wondered to myself how this rather sudden affluence had affected the residents. What would it be like after struggling slowly and laboriously up the ladder of success a step at a time to be suddenly whisked to the top in an express elevator? Just about everybody we met or observed there seemed to be retaining their down to earth set of values that they were brought up with. They were proud of their advancement but not boastful.

The next morning we awoke to a beautiful, sunny day and joined several hundred other people to walk the Azalea Trail, a famous Texas sightseeing experience. We parked our car and walked past many lovely homes and gardens. The homes, in typical Texas manner, sat far back on the property, leaving a large area around the building well-landscaped, formally or otherwise. All the lawns were manicured to perfection.

There were azaleas growing in beds, along pretty little paths, along little brooks, across which were picturesque little arched bridges. Azaleas pervaded the entire scene. Beautiful reds, roses, and whites. They were quite tall, 18 inches to two feet. I guess one could call it a soul satisfying trip. People seemed quieter than usual amidst all the beauty.

Besides the azaleas there were tulips, wisteria and dogwood. We saw quite a little settlement of what were called Sunday houses. They were small, two-story structures with an outside stairway leading to the second floor. In the early days of horse and buggy, families drove into town Saturday. They owned their own Sunday house where they put up for the night, one family had the upstairs and another the downstairs. They would go to church on Sunday and then head home. These places were all in excellent repair and we learned that they were now used for bed and breakfast stopovers.

On our way home early the next morning we passed close by Lake Palestine. A heavy mist was rising from the surface giving it an eerie appearance. It looked as if the tops of the trees were floating above a cloud.

My winters in Texas were most enjoyable. I played bridge with an ever-widening circle of friends, with whom I still keep in touch and occasionally visit when the Wyoming winters exceed their welcome.

Chapter 18

A Full Circle

I was spending a few days in Buffalo and my hostess took a friend and me for a drive to the west edge of town to look at the new Senior Center, an attractive brick building where midday meals were served seven days a week. Adjacent to it were humongous piles of dirt, with bulldozers and trucks scurrying around like ants, rearranging the terrain. "That," said Eva, "will be the new senior apartment building."

My mind was in a turmoil, but not for long. I had made a decision in about two minutes that this would be a great place to live. It was in a good location and was in the town I had always loved. I have always had a special feeling about Buffalo. I remember the spark of excitement I felt as we came over the rise from the north, south or west and got our first view of Buffalo nestled along Clear Creek.

When the senior complex was completed, I made a trip to Buffalo and toured the building with my brother. I was sold immediately so gathered up the required application blanks, which was the first step towards making the move back to Buffalo.

Buffalo Senior Apartments

How simple it would be if I could just say, "I moved to Buffalo the last day of September 1986." Just deciding what to take and what to leave and how to get my possessions over to my new home were going to be major tasks.

Also I needed to make some arrangements for the care of my house, as winter was quickly approaching. Zero temperatures could play havoc with pipes, plumbing and laundry facilities. I had the pipes drained and my neighbors across the street said they would keep an eye on things. But my responsibilities as a homeowner were far from over.

My granddaughter's husband, Craig, loaned his flatbed for the occasion. Another granddaughter, Deena, and her friend drove it over and in an incredibly short time had it loaded and were on their way. Ralph and I loaded up the last few items and were soon ready to leave. I turned to take a last look at my forlorn little house sitting there so empty of items connected with me. No more aroma of fresh baked bread wafting from the kitchen or gathering of vegetables from the garden. I might even miss mowing the yard. For awhile I had a feeling of commiseration that somewhat dampened my enthusiasm, but it wouldn't be entirely deserted, for the neighbors would be faithful caretakers.

Later, after another garage sale and five years of being an absentee landlord, I had an opportunity to sell the house to a lady from Sweden who had married and moved to Wyoming. In a couple of weeks we had all the papers drawn up, signed and the check was in the mail. It was two or three years before I even met the new owners of my house. We were in town one day and met Mr. Saltz, the new owner. He invited us into the house where we met his charming wife and three cute little daughters who served us lemonade and cookies.

They were thoroughly enjoying their new home and in fact were adding two bedrooms. I was happy to find my little house was not forlorn any more but was being treated with love and affection .

When Ralph and I came over the brow of the hill with the last load of my belongings and I glimpsed the Clear Creek Apartments, I felt as if I were coming home, not leaving home. I was surprised and delighted to find that my   granddaughter Deena and her friend   had everything   approximately in its proper place and the place looked homey already.   After a relaxing meal downtown my helpers left for their respective homes and I left for mine.

I sat in my easy chair and surveyed my domain. To the south and east was a green belt which would remain uninhabited as far as buildings were concerned. There was a beautiful view of cottonwood lined Clear Creek as it wound through the valley.   My living room and bedroom face the east so I must go down to the patio to see the magnificent Big Horn Mountains with their snowy peaks.

After a good night's rest I was ready to attack the stacks of boxes piled everywhere.   My daughter came over and took me on a shopping spree. We picked up a heterogeneous supply of gadgetry for the bathroom and kitchen. We then visited the furniture store in search of more substantial items such as a couch, lamps and small rugs. We met and visited with an old friend who, when she learned I was now a Buffaloite, said, "I have need for a substitute for our Tuesday Bridge club. Could you play?" Now bridge has always been one of my favorite pastimes so I accepted with alacrity.

Thus was I launched into the stream of activity that included not only cards but eventually a study club - I know more now about Australia, New Zealand, the economic and political history of our country during the 20th century, and other issues than I had learned in my entire life.

Another interesting group was our senior choir under the direction of our Senior Center Executive

Director, Margaret. We had a most enthusiastic group of members and performed many times at various locations. I served as their piano player, which was a great incentive to improve on my technique.

I had given my piano to Allison as my living room would not accommodate its size, however one time when I was in Denver my son Jim and I went to a music store where I found a Rowland keyboard that would fit nicely in my apartment. What a joy that has been. I have ear phones which allow me to "pull out all the stops," so to speak, and play as long or as loud as I wish.

Ralph and Verna, 1993

I soon discovered a walking path that led from the apartment to Clear Creek and then on west to the Veteran's Home and through town. I love to hike down there. The exercise plus the wonderful fragrant air (a different scent for each season) was like ironing the wrinkles from a garment or combing the tangles from long tresses. A bench placed conveniently near the creek encourages purely idle reflections, the tone being set by the constant mesmerizing sound of the nearby gurgling stream. I always feel invigorated in mind and body as I hike back up the path to face the more mundane duties of homemaking nature.

The Senior Center is one of many conveniences provided for seniors. The nearby YMCA provides aquatic and other types of exercise. The Buffalo Housing supplies seniors with several types of low and moderate-cost living quarters. The Senior bus takes us on errands to stores, doctors, or to any destination in town for a modest fee.

This bus is also made available for more extensive trips. One early fall a group of us went to southern Montana to visit a Hutterite settlement. We drove north to Sheridan then on to Lodgegrass, then to a beautiful valley that showed evidence of an industrious and dedicated citizenry. Nestled down near the river was the little village of 25 Hutterite families.

As we drove into town and down the shady street to our parking place, we saw no decorated store windows, no brick office buildings or schoolhouses or yellow buses. What we did see were a few pedestrians. Mothers with long drab dresses along with their children, girls dressed similar to their mothers with long hair and sturdy shoes and the boys in bib overalls. No bright colors were in evidence.

While we were waiting for the lunch bell to ring we had time to explore the grounds - lovely, well-cared-for lawns. There was a large trough-like vessel containing pemmican - crushed chokecherries and seeds cured in the sunlight. It is a favorite dish for the Indians who buy the finished product. One lady was sitting at an old fashioned spinning wheel spinning natural wool into yarn which they knitted into socks and sweaters.

We saw no cars on the streets of the village, but a pickup was parked down near a pole fence enclosure. It contained a nice load of vegetables, mostly squash and some root crops. We were told later that these industrious farmers and housewives are continually at work making or raising marketable products.

We learned later that their families have a substantial income from this agricultural and domestic output which is not used to buy Ethan Allen furniture or new Oldsmobiles or 20 inch screen TV's, but it is used to buy the best farm land available in the vicinity in order that their sons may have a good solid beginning in running their own farms. This is of course an added incentive for the grown boys to stay home.

We were invited to visit one of the dwellings, a simple, very clean house with necessary furniture but devoid of any embellishments. At this time we were called into the dining room for the noon meal. All the residents ate here together with the cooking being done communally by the women who are marvelous cooks. Their home grown produce is quite prominent on the menu. As we ate a small group of young ladies, all wearing white blouses and long black skirts, sang a few religious songs acappella. There was no sign of a musical instrument anyplace.

The Hutterites make a great attempt to isolate themselves from the outside world, however if professional help is needed they do go outside to seek it. Their children attend school for eight years, learning their basic skills as taught by one of their own eighth grade graduates. Even though these children were provided for materially, it saddened me to think they were denied the opportunity to see great art, architecture, natural wonders or hear great music, famous actors or examine the wonders of science. They are encouraged by their established habits to be satisfied with the status quo, but I wonder if there are not a few inquisitive youngsters who investigate beyond their limited realm.

I would compare their lives to a quiet little river with very few perceptible highs and lows. In our modern world, our lives are more like a wild roaring river dashing over boulders, falling over precipices as waterfalls, sometimes moving almost too fast. We experience peaks of great enjoyment and excitement as well as abysses of disappointment and tough problems. I am sure the latter would develop a deeper character and more interesting personality.

Another interesting trip was to a coal mine in Sheridan County. The mental picture most of us have of a mine is a dark hole in the side of a hill containing rail road tracks leading into the recesses of the mining operation. We saw nothing like that at this mine. The actual mining operation was in plain view.

We watched huge machines remove the overburden from the thick bed of coal which was then loaded onto 200 ton capacity trucks. The trucks hauled the chunks of black shiny coal to the crusher, where after being reduced into more uniform pieces, it is taken to the silo. This structure resembles the structure of the same name used on the farm to store grains.

The coal is dumped onto a conveyer which carries it to the top and dumps it into the hopper. It is then released and drops into a railroad car. A train is moving constantly at a slow speed through the "tunnel" at the bottom of the silo. It takes but a few seconds to load a car which is one of more than a hundred.

Where does all this coal go? Most of it goes to San Antonio or New Jersey to be used in electric generators. This is a twenty-four hour operation going on not only around Sheridan, but there is also a much larger operation in the vicinity of Gillette.

It is truly awesome to see those tons and tons of the earth's surface being carted away. One would think the worked-over terrain would look devastated. Not so. We were driven to a lookout on top of a nearby hill from where we could view the site of a former mine. It had been 100% reclaimed. We saw lovely grassy hills, the grass being better quality than that which grew there previously. Not a blemish to be seen. The only difference not visible but real might have been a slight drop in altitude.

A few years ago the Senior Center sponsored an autumn field trip to Laramie where we boarded a sightseeing train pulled by an old steam engine. We climbed up the steep mountain grade to Centennial and along the mountainside to Fox Park, giving us tremendous views of the precipitous mountain slopes. The dark green of the pine and spruce trees and the spectacular groves of the brilliant aspen trees made a striking contrast.

We chugged along at not more than 20 miles an hour, giving us ample time to observe and snap pictures of the gorgeous array of mountain beauty. When we were on the observation deck we could see the engine ahead as it rounded a curve puffing billows of smoke as it applied "full steam ahead" to get us up a steep grade.

We passed so close to a grove of aspens that one felt it entirely possible to reach out and pluck a leaf as we passed. We came out of the grove of trees to behold a wide open valley. The grassy hillside was broken only by an occasional clump of golden aspen. At the bottom of the valley nestled a small cottage, our first sign of habitation. It looked so idyllic in that setting that it seemed perhaps to be the home of some fairy tale character far removed from our day and age. Our mood changed as we went from the ruggedness of the high altitudes to the serenity of the valley, as if the organ went from "majestic" to "Quasi reverie".

At last it was time to start back to our haven for the night and a chance to stretch our legs. We had time the next morning to visit the territorial prison west of Laramie that was built before the turn of the century and is now a museum. Its structure was a severe style of architecture with no welcoming arches or pillars at the entrance, and was made of dark red brick.

Inside could be seen a bona fide rogues gallery. We looked at pictures of former inmates placed above the cells they had occupied during their internment, along with a description of their crime or crimes. The cells varied in desirability from bad to terrible to abominable judging by the furnishings (quite meager), and the view - from brick wall to a bare glimpse of the outdoors.

We visited the prison chapel where I could not resist sitting down at the organ and playing "The Prisoner's Song." We went across a lane and had a look at their broom factory, where the less violent inmates had worked at making brooms. There was also a blacksmith shop where some of them had worked.

Our drive to Cheyenne gave us an opportunity to visit the magnificent Lincoln memorial atop Sherman

Hill, which was sculpted by a local well-known sculptor, Robert Russin. Nearby is an older but impressive monument in honor of the Ames brothers, railroad pioneers responsible for the beginning of the Union Pacific Railroad.

It was starting to spit snow by this time and we were glad when we reached Little America, a great place for a reststop. I had made previous arrangements with Jim to meet me there. I left the bus group and went on to Denver with Jim for a week. A trip to Denver is always a treat, from the large shopping emporiums and show places to the quiet beauty of their summer cabin on the banks of Fall River up in the mountains.

In Denver I am always assured of pleasant experiences: material, aesthetic, and gastronomic, all enhanced by kindred congeniality.

How wonderful it is to live in the age of travel, made easy even for very senior citizens. It is our choice however. There is so much to see in this marvelous world of ours that we need to take advantage of every trail available to us, and see and hear as much as we can of the wondrous works of man: architecture, art, highways, and even more important the unsurpassable works of nature.

As we look back on the 20th century, we might call it a period of revolution in a good sense. We saw drastic changes in our living environment and habits.

Today we zip across the continent in hours, compared to days, weeks, or even months, as in the first quarter of the century (depending on the mode of travel). In those days mail would arrive at its destination no faster than the vehicle carrying it. Today via computer and e-mail, we are able to send our own message half way around the world in a matter of seconds.

Tremendous advances in time and energy-saving devices have been made in many fields that have affected people in all walks of life, from the factory worker to the homemaker. In spite of all of this, everybody complains of not having enough time.

What became of all this time we were supposed to have saved? There are many forces at work that provide games, entertainment and constructive activities in an attempt to keep everyone busy - from children to senior citizens. Time to be alone, time to contemplate, is a rare commodity.

It would be interesting to see a trend toward ideas requiring brain power, without so much dependence on machines. How about a return to the "Age of Reason" for the 21st century?

Whatever the next century brings, I wake up each morning knowing something will happen to make that day better than the one before.